**Upper Elementary Level**
**Textbook for Children**
**Ages 9-12 Years**

# Teachings of the Qur'ān

**Volume Two**

Tahreem Akhtar

Abidullah Ghazi
Tasneema Khatoon Ghazi

IQRA'
International Educational Foundation
Chicago

# Part of a Comprehensive and Systematic Program of Islamic Studies

**A Textbook for Qur'anic Studies Elementary Level**

**Teachings of the Quran, Part Two**
First Limited Edition

**Chief Program Editors**
Dr. Abidullah al-Ansari Ghazi
(Ph.D. History of Religion, Harvard University)

Dr. Tasneema Ghazi
(Ph.D. Curriculum-Reading, University of Minnesota)

**Reviewers:**
Fadel Abdallah
(M.A. Islamic Studies, University of Minnesota)

Dr. Assad N. Busool
(Ph.D. Arabic and Islamic Studies, University of California, Berkeley)

Maulana Shu'aib ud-Din
(Faḍil Dar ul-Ulum, Karachi)

Maulana Obaid Ullah Saleem
(Faḍil Dar ul-Ulum, Deoband)

**Language Editors:**
Dr. Khwaja Moinul Hassan
(Ph.D. English, Purdue University)

Noura Durkee
(M.A. Fine Arts, Stanford University)

**Art Direction & Design**
Jennifer Mazzoni
(B.A. Illustration, Columbia College Chicago)



Second printing 1997
Third Printing May 2001
Cedar graphics, USA



**IQRA' International Educational Foundation,**
**7450 Skokie Blvd., Skokie, IL 60077**
**Tel: 847-673-4072; Fax: 847-673-4095**
**email: iqra@aol.com**
**website: www.iqra.org**

Library of Congress Catalog Card Number 92-248962
ISBN # 1-56316-104-4

بِسْمِ اللَّهِ الرَّحْمَٰنِ الرَّحِيمِ

وَلَقَدْ يَسَّرْنَا الْقُرْآنَ لِلذِّكْرِ فَهَلْ مِن مُّدَّكِرٍ

And in truth We have made
the Qur'ān easy to remember;
but is there any that remembers?
*(Al-Qamar 54:17)*

**Dedicated to:**

**The Huffaẓ Ṣaḥabah**
**of**
**Rasūlullāh, *Ṣalla Allāhu 'alai-hi wa Sallam***
**who were first to**
**memorize the Qur'ān**
**as it was revealed**

1. 'Abdullāh Ibn Mas'ūd
2. Mu'ādh Ibn Jabal
3. Zaid Ibn Thābit
4. Ḥudhaifah
5. 'Abū Mūsa Al-'Ash'arī
6. 'Abū Hurairah
7. 'Abu Ad-Dardā'
8. 'Abdullāh 'Ibn 'Abbās
9. 'Abdullāh 'Ibn 'Amr Ibn Al-'Ās
10. 'Abdullāh Ibn 'Umar
11. 'Abdullah Ibn Az-Zubair
12. Talḥah Ibn Az-Zubair
13. 'Ubādah Ibn Aṣ-Ṣāmit
14. Sa'd Ibn Abī Waqqāṣ
15. 'Abdullah Ibn Aṣ-Ṣā'ib
16. Fuḍālah Ibn 'Ubaid
17. Sa'īd Ibn 'Ubaid
18. Maslamah Ibn Mukhlid
19. 'Ubayy Ibn Ka'b
20. Majma' Ibn Jāriyah
21. 'Abū Zaid Ibn As-Sakan
22. Sālim Ibn Ma'qal
23. 'A'ishah, Mother of the Believers
24. Ḥafṣah, daughter of 'Abū Bakr
25. 'Umm Salmah
26. Hind Bint 'Abi 'Umayyah

***Riḍwān Allah 'alai-him 'Ajma'in***
**(May Allah be pleased with them all.)**

---

As quoted in Dr. Ahmad Sakr; *Islamic Lists*

IQRA's Note

## TO PARENTS AND TEACHERS

All praises are due to Allah (SWT) and choicest blessing be on Muhammad, *Salla Allahu`alaihi wa Sallam,* the final Messenger who came with the final Revelation, the Qur'an, and who is a light and guidance for all of humankind.

Iqra' International Educational Foundation is grateful to Allah (SWT) for enabling it to complete this unique work, Teachings of the Qur'an (Volumes 1, II, III), textbooks of Qur'anic Studies at the Elementary level. This is an attempt which is unique in its presentation and thorough in its application. These three textbooks represent years of hard work in research and application of modern methodology to the teachings of the Qur'an for young children.

Teachings of the Qur'an, in three volumes, introduces young children to the entire range of the message of the Qur'an at their level of understanding. The authors apply the same, well-tested methodology which has given their *Sīrah* Program (at Elementary, Junior and Senior levels) a great success and worldwide acclaim. These textbooks, along with the companion volume *Short Surahs,* represent the first systematic attempt to introduce the message of the Qur'an to elementary age children.

IQRA's Comprehensive Program of Qur'anic Studies is, like the Program of *Sīrah,* being produced at four levels and is under final editing and publication.

The following points regarding these textbooks should be especially noted by the readers:

- These books are a part of **IQRA's Comprehensive and Systematic Program of Islamic Studies** at four levels: Preschool, Elementary, Junior and Senior. More than fifty scholars, educators and professionals are busy in producing this program. So far over eighty books have been produced. The complete program is expected to have over three hundred books; the most comprehensive library of Islamic books and educational material for our children and youth.

- This volume of Teachings of the Qur'ān deals with the teaching of the Qur'ān on Islamic *'Akhlāq,* the **Islamic code of morals, manners and ethics:** Its three sections deal with the Qur'anic perspective on:

i. the Foundations of Islamic *'Akhlāq*
ii. the Right Actions (to be followed) and
iii. Wrong Actions (to be avoided).

✧ Each lesson starts with an *'Āyah,* which is selected to give the message of the Qur'ān on that subject.

✧ The *'Āyah* is first written in Arabic and then transliterated into English to help the child with correct pronunciation. It is advisable that the child reads this *'Āyah* in Arabic with the help of a teacher of Qur'ānic Studies, avoiding transliteration as much as possible.

✧ The meaning of the *'Āyah* is provided in simple language.

✧ The vocabulary of each word of the *'Āyah* is explained in Appendix I, to help those students who want to pursue further study of the Qur'ān through translation. Such an exercise would greatly help the understanding of the Qur'ān and facilitate the learning of Arabic. These books are also **an integral part of Iqra's comprehensive program of Arabic studies** which aims to systematically teach Arabic as a second language from an early age.

✧ The EXPLANATION which follows explains the message of the *'Āyah* in short simple sentences. The explanation covers not only the selected *'Āyah* but the general theme of the Qur'ān on that subject.

✧ At the end of each lesson the basic message of the Qur'ān on that subject is repeated in three short sentences for reinforcement under: WE HAVE LEARNED.

✧ A list of new and difficult words are restated at the end of each lesson under: DO WE KNOW THESE WORDS.

✧ A glossary of the difficult words is provided at the end of the book.

✧ Workbooks based on the pattern of *Sīrah* program are under publication to provide reinforcement and develop educational skills further.

Iqra' International's effort's in the field of Islamic studies is unique, systematic and comprehensive. We urge you to support this effort by joining: IQRA' BOOK CLUB, and the ranks of 'ANṢĀRS OF IQRA' EDUCATIONAL PROGRAM by contributing (tax deductible) each year to establish IQRA' FOUNDATION as the foremost center of Islamic Education in the West.

Chief Editors
27 February 1995 *27 Ramaḍan al-Mubarak 1415*

بِسْمِ اللّٰهِ الرَّحْمٰنِ الرَّحِيْمِ

# Table of Contents

بِسْمِ اللّٰهِ الرَّحْمٰنِ الرَّحِيْمِ

Table of Contents

بسم الله الرحمن الرحيم

# IQRA'
# ARABIC TRANSLITERATION CHART

| | | | | | | | | |
|---|---|---|---|---|---|---|---|---|
| q | ق | * | z | ز | | ' | أء | * |
| k | ك | | s | س | | b | ب | |
| l | ل | | sh | ش | | t | ت | |
| m | م | | s | ص | * | th | ث | * |
| n | ن | | d | ض | * | j | ج | |
| h | ه | | t | ط | * | h | ح | * |
| w | و | | z | ظ | * | kh | خ | * |
| y | ي | | ' | ع | * | d | د | |
| | | | gh | غ | * | dh | ذ | * |
| | | | f | ف | | r | ر | |

| SHORT VOWELS | LONG VOWELS | DIPHTHONGS |
|---|---|---|
| a \ ـَ | a \ ـَا | aw \ ـَوْ |
| u \ ـُ | u \ ـُو | ai \ ـَيْ |
| i \ ـِ | i \ ـِي | |
| Such as: *kataba* كَتَبَ | Such as: *Kitab* كِتَاب | Such as: *Lawh* لَوْح |
| Such as: *Qul* قُلْ | Such as: *Mamnun* مَمْنُون | Such as: *'Ain* عَيْن |
| Such as: *Ni'mah* نِعْمَة | Such as: *Din* دِين | |

* Special attention should be given to the symbols marked with stars for they have no equivalent in the English sounds .

*** *Special Note on the Transliteration of Words Involving the Definite Article* (ال)**

- There are situations where the alif ( ا ) of the Definite Article is not pronounced though it is present in writing. To account for this type of 'Alif in the transliteration system, we have added an (a) in parenthesis before the Lam.(ال)

Example :

Al-Hamdu li Allahi Rabbi al-'Alamin, is written as
Al-Hamdu li-(A)llahi Rabbi (a)l-Alamin, and read as
Al-Hamdu li-llahi Rabbi-l-'Alamin

# ISLAMIC INVOCATIONS:

Rasūlullāh, *Ṣalla Allahu 'alaihi wa Sallam* (صَلَّى ٱللَّهُ عَلَيْهِ وَسَلَّم), and the Qur'ān teach us to glorify Allah (SWT) when we mention His Name and to invoke His Blessings when we mention the names of His Angels, Messengers, the *Ṣaḥābah* and the Pious Ancestors.

When we mention the Name of Allah we must say: *Subḥāna-hū Wa-Ta'ālā* (سُبْحَانَهُ وَتَعَالَىٰ), Glorified is He and High. In this book we write (SWT) to remind us to Glorify Allah.

When we mention the name of Rasūlullāh (S) we must say: *Ṣalla Allāhu 'alai-hi wa-Sallam,* (صَلَّى ٱللَّهُ عَلَيْهِ وَسَلَّم), May Allah's Blessings and Peace be upon him.
We write an (Ṣ) to remind us to invoke Allah's Blessings on Rasūlullāh.

When we mention the name of an angel or a prophet we must say: *Alai-hi-(a)s-Salām* (عَلَيْهِ ٱلسَّلاَم), Upon him be peace.
We write an (A) to remind us to involе Allah's Peace upon him.

When we hear the name of the *Ṣaḥābah* we must say:
For more than two, *Raḍiya-(A)llāhu Ta'ālā 'an-hum* (رَضِيَ ٱللَّهُ تَعَالَىٰ عَنْهُمْ), May Allah be pleased with them.
For two of them, *Raḍiya-(A)llāhu Ta'ālā 'an-humā* (رَضِيَ ٱللَّهُ تَعَالَىٰ عَنْهُمَا), May Allah be pleased with both of them.
For a *Ṣaḥābī*, *Raḍiya-(A)llāhu Ta'ālā 'an-hu* (رَضِيَ ٱللَّهُ تَعَالَىٰ عَنْهُ), May Allah be pleased with him.
For a *Ṣaḥābiyyah*, *Raḍiya-(A)llāhu Ta'ālā 'an-hā* (رَضِيَ ٱللَّهُ تَعَالَىٰ عَنْهَا), May Allah be pleased with her.
We write (R) to remind us to invoke Allah's Pleasure with a *Ṣaḥābī,* a *Sahabiyah* or with *Ṣaḥābah.*

When we hear the name of the Pious Ancestor *(As-Salaf as-Ṣāliḥ)* we must say.
For a man, *Raḥmatu-(A)llāh 'alai-hi* (رَحْمَةُ ٱللَّهِ عَلَيْهِ), May Allah's Mercy be upon him.
For a woman, *Raḥmatu-(A)llāh 'alai-hā* (رَحْمَةُ ٱللَّهِ عَلَيْهَا), May Allah's Mercy be with her.

# Section I

# Foundation of Islamic *'Akhlāq*

Lesson 1

# What is 'Akhlāq?

بِسْمِ اللّٰهِ الرَّحْمٰنِ الرَّحِيْمِ

*'Akhlāq* are the rules of morals and manners that we must practice in our relationship with others. Islamic *'Akhlāq* provides the basis for a Muslim's behavior in society. Islam offers an ideal code of behavior for people to follow in their relations with other human beings. This Islamic code of behavior is more complete and comprehensive than any other offered by any other religion or society.

In English, we use two terms for *'Akhlāq:* ethical behavior, or morals and manners. To have morals or ethics is to be able to differentiate right behavior from wrong. If we lack *'Akhlāq,* we cannot form a peaceful and civilized society.

Every society throughout the world has a code of behavior *('Akhlāq)* that it must follow in its daily interactions. This includes everything from city laws for automobiles and pedestrians, to dress codes in the work place and classroom rules in school.

These rules are made by each society to make life easy for everyone. It is the moral duty for every citizen to follow these rules. Every society also has rules of moral behavior that come from religion and its traditions. People follow these rules because these were taught by prophets and religious teachers and have been accepted by the society.

The rules of Islamic *'Akhlāq* are revealed to us by Allah (SWT) and taught to us through the *Sunnah* of Rasūlullāh (S). Islamic *'Akhlāq* teaches us what is right and what is wrong. The code of Isla-mic *'Akhlāq* is clearly laid down in the Qur'ān and the *Sirah* of Rasūlullāh (S).

As human beings, all of us must learn what is right and what is wrong. Within our families, we must learn both our duties as husbands, wives, sons or daughters, and know what our responsibilities are as mothers or fathers. One person may carry many positions within his or her family and may often be required to act in different ways to fulfill those responsibilities.

As human beings, we first learn to live with our families and relatives. Soon we learn to deal with our neighbors, friends and colleagues. Often, however, we deal with total strangers. All of these people expect us to behave well with them, just as we expect them to behave well with us.

Most moral codes are unwritten rules that people have followed for generations. All human beings have certain responsibilities towards others and we must fulfill them. Unfortunately, there are some people in the world who do not respect these moral codes of behavior. Such people cause problems for others and make everyone's life difficult. To stop these evil people, the societies make rules and laws, and enforce them through police and courts of law.

Some societies, however, have made one set of rules for themselves and another set for other groups of people. This is unfair and causes inequality between different groups of people.

Some people even believe that they have a special relationship with God, or are His special creation, therefore, deserve better treatment than others. They have invented stories to suit their own interests.

The Islamic moral code does not favor one group of people over another. It builds a human society which is based on human equality and justice for all. Islamic *'Akhlāq* teaches us how we must behave toward other people, be they our relatives or strangers, be they Muslim or non-Muslim.

## WE HAVE LEARNED:

* *'Akhlāq* are the code of moral rules and ethical regulations that each society has made for its people to live by.

* Societies make laws and establish punishments for those who break their laws.

* Some societies believe in their own superiority and make special laws for themselves.

## DO WE KNOW THESE WORDS?

*'Akhlāq*
civilized
exclusive
interaction
morals and manners
prescribed
responsibility
social behavior

Lesson 2

# Sources of Islamic *'Akhlāq*

بِسْمِ اللَّهِ الرَّحْمَٰنِ الرَّحِيمِ

The source of all moral rules and ethical principles, according to Islam, is the same for all people; the Divine Guidance. Allah (SWT) has sent His Guidance to all the people of the world to teach them *Tawḥīd* (The Oneness of Allah) and the moral codes of life. Allah (SWT) sent this Guidance throughout the world, by means of different Prophets *('Anbiyā')* and Messengers *(Rusul)* throughout the ages. This is why most human societies worldwide have many moral rules in common.

Allah (SWT) has created all human beings on the *Fiṭrah,* the true and pure nature. All human beings have an inborn sense of right and wrong and most people want to follow the right path. Societies have also evolved many rules to make life easier and more orderly. Societies develop these rules to make life easy for everyone.

The rules such as driving on specified sides of the road, fixing times for a standard workday, rules for garbage cleaning, speed limits for the roads, fixing one-way or two-way streets, forming lines to await one's turn, etc. are designed to facilitate life for everyone. Since such rules are made to benefit everyone, to follow them becomes our moral duty. If we do not do so, we may bring inconvenience and danger to ourselves and to others.

Some moral rules are made into law by societies, and anyone who breaks them may be punished. The best reason for a Muslim to follow the moral rules is to please Allah (SWT) and to help other human beings.

Some people follow them only out of fear of punishment. If they feel that no one is watching them, they do not mind breaking the rules. Such people do not realize that Allah (SWT) is always watching them. A true Muslim must always follow the rules of Islamic *'Akhlāq* and the rules and laws of one's society, whether he is by himself or working with others.

As Muslims, we believe that Allah (SWT) is the Creator of all, and that He has sent Divine Guidance to every human being through His Messengers. As fellow human beings, we all share the same basic human rights, and in the *'Ākhirah* (the Hereafter), Allah (SWT) will judge us according to our faith and actions.

The Qur'ān guides us in all matters, whether they deal with our personal lives, our family matters or with social relations. Islam teaches us what rules we must follow and must not follow in our lives.

The Qur'ān teaches us that, as individuals and as a community, we must practice righteousness, and lead others to the right path. We must also cooperate with other people of goodwill in those things that are good and beneficial for all.

The Qur'ān also lays down that, as individuals and as a community, we should not practice evil and we should forbid others from practicing it. We must never cooperate in those things that are sinful and harmful to others.

The life of Rasūlullāh (S) is the best example for us and his *Sunnah* is the true guide for all our actions. No other people have been blessed with such a clear Guidance as we Muslims are. We have a special responsibility to follow the moral teachings of our religion and be an example of Islamic *'Akhlāq* for everyone.

## Firm Foundations

Rasūlullāh (S) has left best guides for us to follow. He says: "I am leaving with you two things, if you hold fast to them you shall never go astray. And that is the Book of Allah and the *Sunnah* of His Prophet." *(At-Targhib wa-(a)t-Tarhīb)*

*('Abū Hurairah - Mishkāt Al-Maṣābīḥ)*

## WE HAVE LEARNED:

* Divine Guidance is the source of all *'Akhlāq*.
* Human societies have also evolved rules for their convenience.
* The Qur'an and the *Sunnah* are the two basic and complete sources of Islamic *'Akhlāq*.

## DO WE KNOW THESE WORDS?

*'Anbiyā'*
convenience
Divine Guidance
evolve
inborn sense
righteousness
*Rusul*

# Lesson 3

# Foundations of Islamic *'Akhlāq*

Islam offers us the most complete code of *'Akhlāq,* which teaches us how to behave in our dealings and relationships with others. Islam also teaches us the reasoning behind our behavior, so we know why we should or should not do certain things.

Islamic *'Akhlāq* is based upon certain basic ideas; we must understand these ideas to appreciate the Islamic teachings on *'Akhlāq*. We have discussed basic Islamic teachings in detail in the previous volume. Here, we sum up those teachings in relation to Islamic *'Akhlāq*.

Islamic *'Akhlāq* is based upon three basic principles: *Tawḥīd* (the Oneness of Allah), the *Risālah* (the mission of the Messengers) and the *'Ākhirah* (the Hereafter).

By definition, *Tawḥīd* is the belief that there is only one God, Allah (SWT). He is the Creator and Supporter of all. He has created us and sent us to this world with a purpose and to Him we shall return. Everything in this world is His creation, and He is the Lord of everyone. He has created all human beings and has given them knowledge and wisdom so that they may choose the right path. Every individual is thus responsible for his own actions.

He has created all human beings from a single couple, *'Ādam* (A) and *Ḥawwā'* (R). No single individual is preferred over another by Allah (SWT) except through his *Taqwā,* the Righteousness. Every human being has been given the power of choice between good and evil.

Allah (SWT) is Merciful, Loving and Kind and wants to help human beings. It is because of this love that He sent Messengers to guide human beings towards Him.

Islamic *'Akhlāq* covers every aspect of life and to follow it is to obey Allah's plan on Earth. Allah (SWT) has sent His Guidance through His Prophets to all the people of the world. All Messengers and Prophets taught their people Allah's Religion, Islam, and showed, through their example, how to practice it.

Some Messengers received Books of Guidance from Allah (SWT) in the form of Revelations. Prophet Muḥammad (S) was sent as the last Messenger of Allah (SWT). He received the Qur'ān as the final Book of Allah (SWT). Islam is the last and most complete Message of Allah (SWT) and has the best and most complete system of Islamic *'Akhlāq*.

Allah (SWT) as the Lord and Creator of everything gives everyone a chance to accept His religion and follow His path. Islam is the only religion for all human beings. Islam is not for any specific group or race of people. Anyone who accepts Islam becomes a Muslim.

In the *'Ākhirah,* the Hereafter, we shall all be brought before Allah (SWT) and judged for our actions. Our power, influence, position, language, color, race or country will not help us. In the *'Ākhirah,* nothing except our own faith and actions, and Allah's Mercy, will help us.

Allah (SWT) wants Muslims to be an example of good morals and beautiful manners. A Muslim follows the code of Islamic *'Akhlāq* to please Allah (SWT); he does not do so to gain the favors of others.

## Du'a' of Rasūlullāh

O Allah, I ask you for good health with right faith, and right faith with best *'Akhlāq* (morals and manners).
I ask you for the success of this world which ensures a true success and mercy from you in the Hereafter. And I ask you for security, forgiveness and pleasure.
*(Aṭ-Ṭabrāni, Hakim)*

## WE HAVE LEARNED:

* Islam gives us the most complete code of *'Akhlāq*.
* The teachings of the Qur'ān and the *Sunnah* of Rasūlullāh (S) are the only guide to Islamic *'Akhlāq*.
* The *Tawḥīd,* the *Risālah* and the *'Ākhirah* are the basis of Islamic *'Akhlāq*.

## DO WE KNOW THESE WORDS?

appreciate
purpose
*Ar-Risālah*
*Tawḥīd*
worldly
*Ḥawwā'*

# Lesson 4

# Personal Responsibility

بِسْمِ ٱللَّهِ ٱلرَّحْمَٰنِ ٱلرَّحِيمِ

وَلَا تَقْفُ مَا لَيْسَ لَكَ بِهِۦ عِلْمٌ
إِنَّ ٱلسَّمْعَ وَٱلْبَصَرَ وَٱلْفُؤَادَ كُلُّ
أُو۟لَٰٓئِكَ كَانَ عَنْهُ مَسْـُٔولًا

*Wa lā taqfu mā laisa la-ka bi-hī ʿilmun,*
*ʻinn-(a)s-samʻa wa-(a)l-baṣara wa-(a)l-fuʼāda kullu*
*ʻulāʻika kāna ʻan-hu masʼūlā*

And follow not that of which you have no knowledge;
for every hearing, seeing and feeling (in the heart); all these
will be questioned (on the Day of Judgment).
(*'Al-'Isra'* 17:36)

EXPLANATION:

Everything we have, whether it be our bodies, our abilities or our worldly possessions, is a trust from Allah (SWT). This trust must be safeguarded and used according to His commands. Since this trust has been established with Allah (SWT), we must use these blessings according to His wishes.

Every human being has been given this trust, but not everyone chooses to safeguard it according to the wishes of Allah (SWT). Sometimes, when people possess something, they begin thinking that they really own it and that they can do whatever they want with it. They use these gifts of Allah (SWT) for their own benefit without giving due praise to Him for these blessings.

Their successes and achievements, instead of making them thankful, make them proud and arrogant. The more these people achieve success, the more they believe in their own merits and forget about the Mercy of Allah (SWT). It is important to remember to thank Him for the blessings.

Allah (SWT) has given us beautiful bodies and healthy minds which we use to work and think with. Through our eyes, ears, tongues and minds we gain knowledge of this world. Our bodies and minds are a trust from Allah (SWT).

Allah (SWT) has made human beings responsible creatures. We are the only creation which has such a high level of intelligence. If we do not use our various faculties – hearing, vision and feeling – properly, we shall be answerable to Allah (SWT) on the Day of Judgment.

We are the only ones that have the ability to differentiate between right and wrong. The knowledge that we are unable to gain through our bodies and senses has been taught to us through His *Waḥi,* or the Revelation. He has sent His Messengers to guide us and He has given us His Books to teach us right from wrong.

Seeking knowledge is an obligation which Islam has enjoined upon every Muslim. The Qur'ān teaches us the beautiful Du'ā':

وَقُل رَّبِّ زِدْنِي عِلْمًا

Oh my Lord, increase me in knowledge.
(*Ṭāhā* 20:114)

We should not follow those things of which we have no knowledge. Our minds, eyes, ears and tongues must not be used for any evil purpose. Rasulūllāh (S) used to pray to Allah (SWT):

"O Allah, bless me with the knowledge that helps everyone. O Allah, save me from the knowledge that harms others."

## WE HAVE LEARNED:

* Every blessing that Allah (SWT) has given us is a trust.
* Allah (SWT) has created human beings as a responsible creation.
* The true purpose of our creation is to serve Allah (SWT).

## DO WE KNOW THESE WORDS?

arrogance
differentiate
imposed
faculties
merit
pride

# Lesson 5

# Family Responsibility

بِسۡمِ ٱللَّهِ ٱلرَّحۡمَٰنِ ٱلرَّحِيمِ

يَٰٓأَيُّهَا ٱلَّذِينَ ءَامَنُواْ قُوٓاْ أَنفُسَكُمۡ
وَأَهۡلِيكُمۡ نَارٗا وَقُودُهَا ٱلنَّاسُ وَٱلۡحِجَارَةُ

*Ya-'ayyuha-(a)lladhīna 'āmanū qū 'anfusa-kum*
*wa 'ahlī-kum nāran waqūdu-ha-(a)n-nāsu wa-(a)l-ḥijaratu....*

"O you who believe, save yourself and your families from
Fire whose fuel is men and stones. . ."
(*'At-Taḥrīm* 66:6)

EXPLANATION:

Most of our time is spent towards improving the lives of our family members and in trying to find better opportunities and comforts for them. We love and care for our families, and want to provide them with the best comforts and conveniences of life that we can.

Parents work hard to support their families and take care of all of their children's needs. Not everyone is fortunate enough to have the resources necessary to take care of his family's needs. All parents, whether rich or poor, work very hard to make the life of their children better and more comfortable.

The Qur'ān enjoins upon us the responsibility of saving our children from the Fire of Hell. We can save our families by teaching our children the religion of Islam and showing them how to practice it. Teaching children *'Adab,* good Islamic behavior, is better than all the comforts parents could offer them.

Allah (SWT) gives us children and wealth as a test and trial in this world. The Qur'an says:

فِتۡنَةٞۚ وَٱللَّهُ عِندَهُۥٓ أَجۡرٌ عَظِيمٞ

Indeed, your wealth and your children
are a test, whereas with Allah is the highest reward.
*('At-Taghābun 64:15)*

Not all parents are wealthy. Some of those who cannot provide for their children, offer them for sale to the wealthy, or abandon them, or kill them. The Qur'ān forbids this completely:

وَلَا تَقْتُلُوٓا۟ أَوْلَـٰدَكُمْ خَشْيَةَ إِمْلَـٰقٍ ۖ نَّحْنُ نَرْزُقُهُمْ وَإِيَّاكُمْ ۚ إِنَّ قَتْلَهُمْ كَانَ خِطْـًٔا كَبِيرًا

Do not kill your children fearing poverty,
We shall provide for them as well as for you,
Indeed, the killing of them is a great sin.
*('Al-'Isrā' 17:31)*

Many Arab parents before the time of Rasūlullāh (S) buried their daughters alive. Islam forbids this completely. Most people preferred the sons over their daughters. Allah (SWT) blessed Rasūlullāh (S) with four daughters. He showed us how to raise daughters and love them.

Muslim parents are asked by Allah (SWT) to take good care of their families, give them good Islamic education and teach them *Islamic 'Akhlaq*. By living and dying as a Muslim, one is saved from the Fire of Hell.

As Muslims, we should help our parents in this world and be a comfort for them in the Hereafter. Rasūlullāh (S) said that a pious son who remembers his parents in his Du'ā', and through his good deeds, is a *Ṣadaqah Jāriyah* for the parents in the *'Ākhirah.*

## Raising a Girl

Rasūlullāh (S) said: "If a girl is born to someone, and he did not bury her as in the Days of Ignorance, nor looked at her with contempt, nor preferred his sons over her, Allah will admit him to *Jannah.*"
*('Abū Dāwūd)*

## WE HAVE LEARNED:

* Parents must save themselves and their children from the Fire of Hell.
* Good Islamic education and teaching of *'Adab* is better than all the comforts we can offer our families.
* A pious child who remembers parents in his Du'ā' benefits his parents, even in their graves.

## DO WE KNOW THESE WORDS?

*'Adab*
Days of Ignorance
investment
*Ṣadaqah*
*Ṣadaqah Jāriyah*
abandon

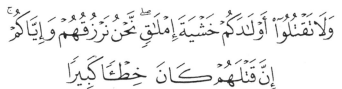

بِسْمِ ٱللَّهِ ٱلرَّحْمَٰنِ ٱلرَّحِيمِ

وَءَاتِ ذَا ٱلْقُرْبَىٰ حَقَّهُۥ وَٱلْمِسْكِينَ
وَٱبْنَ ٱلسَّبِيلِ وَلَا تُبَذِّرْ تَبْذِيرًا

*Wa-'āti dha-(a)l-qurbā ḥaqqa-hū wa-(a)l-miskīna*
*wa-(i)bna-(a)s-sabīli, wa-' lā tubadhdhir tabdhīrā(n)*

And give the relatives their due rights, as well as
to the needy, and to the traveller,
and waste not your wealth in wasteful manner.
(*'Al-'Isrā'* 17:26)

EXPLANATION:

It is Allah (SWT) Who has given us all that we have, and in return, He asks us to be generous and giving. Thus, giving to others is one way of thanking Allah (SWT). Allah (SWT) says:

لَئِن شَكَرْتُمْ لَأَزِيدَنَّكُمْ

If you will thank Me,
I will increase (My blessings) for you.
*('Ibrāhīm 14:7)*

As Believers, we know that all that we have has been provided by Allah (SWT). Many of the blessings of Allah (SWT) are free and we do not even have to work for them. We cannot live without air and Allah (SWT) has provided us with it in abundance. The Sun provides us with necessary light on a daily basis. Water is an important source of life and Allah (SWT) has covered most of the Earth's surface with water for us.

There are many things that we must work hard for. The final outcome of our work is decided by Allah (SWT). We should always work hard and leave the results of our efforts to Allah (SWT).

Allah (SWT) has made it an obligation on us to take care of others. The Qur'ān commands us to specially take care of our relatives and to give them their rightful share in inheritance and help them in their needs.

The needy and the traveller do not have a legal right over us, but Allah (SWT) has still made it an obligation on us to take care of them. One way of thanking Allah (SWT) is to spend our money in His Path.

Whatever reward we do not get in this life for our good actions, we are sure to get in the Hereafter. We should always desire our reward in the Hereafter instead of in this life, because this life is short, whereas that of the Hereafter is eternal.

The Qur'ān speaks of the Believers:

وَمِمَّا رَزَقْنَٰهُمْ يُنفِقُونَ

And they spend (on others) of what
We have given them.
*('Al-Baqarah 2:3)*

Some people hoard their money and others waste it on useless things. Both of these people are disliked by Allah (SWT). Sharing our money and property with others is much better than hoarding it or wasting it. Whatever is left after our needs are fulfilled should be spent to fulfill the needs of others.

## Caring for the Relatives

إِنَّ ٱللَّهَ يَأْمُرُ بِٱلْعَدْلِ وَٱلْإِحْسَٰنِ

وَإِيتَآيِ ذِى ٱلْقُرْبَىٰ

Indeed! Allah commands justice, kindness
and giving relatives their due.
*('An-Naḥl 16:90)*

## WE HAVE LEARNED:

* It is our duty as Muslims to take care of the needs of others.
* It is not right to hoard or waste our wealth, while the needs of so many people remain unfulfilled.
* Allah (SWT) always helps those who help others.

## DO WE KNOW THESE WORDS?

ample
generous
hoard
obligation
wayfarer

Lesson 7

# Obligations to Parents

بِسۡمِ اللّٰهِ الرَّحۡمٰنِ الرَّحِيۡمِ

وَقَضَىٰ رَبُّكَ أَلَّا تَعۡبُدُوٓاْ إِلَّآ إِيَّاهُ
وَبِٱلۡوَٰلِدَيۡنِ إِحۡسَٰنًاۚ إِمَّا يَبۡلُغَنَّ عِندَكَ ٱلۡكِبَرَ
أَحَدُهُمَآ أَوۡ كِلَاهُمَا فَلَا تَقُل لَّهُمَآ
أُفّٖ وَلَا تَنۡهَرۡهُمَا وَقُل لَّهُمَا قَوۡلٗا كَرِيمٗا

*Wa-qaḍā Rabbu-ka al-lā ta'būdū 'illa 'iyyā-hu wa-bi-*
*(a)l-wālidaini 'iḥsāna(n) 'immā yablughanna 'inda-ka-(a)l-kibara*
*'aḥadu-huma 'aw kilā-humā wa-la taqul-la-humā*
*'uffin wa la-tanhar-humā wa qul la-huma qawlan karīmā*

And your Lord commands you to worship none other
except Him and that you be kind to parents.
If any one of them, or both of them, reach old age in
your life, say not to them a word of contempt, nor rebuke
them, but speak to them gracious word.
*('Al-'Isrā' 17:23)*

EXPLANATION:

The Qur'ān teaches us two most important things: Firstly, we must worship only Allah (SWT) and secondly, we must always be kind to our parents.

No believing human being can deny the importance of worshiping Allah (SWT). The Qur'ān emphasizes the importance of serving the parents by linking it with the worship of Allah (SWT). This shows how important in Islam it is to respect, love and serve our parents.

Our mothers gave birth to us and our fathers love us and care for us. Our parents raised us, taught us good manners and cared for our happiness and comfort. We must always be gentle and respectful to our parents, even if we disagree with them sometimes.

Allah (SWT) has placed the love and care for children in the hearts of their parents. When parents are young, they do their best for us. When they become older, they get weaker and are sick more often. At this time, they need the same care and love from their children that they had given to them.

When children grow older, accept challenging jobs, get married and have children of their own, they may often forget their duty towards their parents. We must always be patient and show kindness to our parents. We should remember how kind our parents had been to us when we were young. The Qur'ān advises us further:

وَٱخْفِضْ لَهُمَا جَنَاحَ ٱلذُّلِّ مِنَ ٱلرَّحْمَةِ وَقُل
رَّبِّ ٱرْحَمْهُمَا كَمَا رَبَّيَانِى صَغِيرًا

—And, out of kindness, lower to them wings of
humility and pray (to Allah) for them saying;
My Lord have Mercy on both of them
as they did care for me when I was young.
*('Al-'Isrā' 17:24)*

The lowering of wings of humility means to obey our parents, be kind to them and to always be generous to them. Some of the ways we can honor our parents are by:

- Greeting them each morning and when they return from work with a smile and say *'Assalamu 'Alai-kum.*
- Helping them in their work.
- Spending some time with them and talking to them about ourselves and asking about them.
- Buying them gifts from our own money on special occasions.
- Taking special care of them when they are sick, or grow old.
- Doing some chores for them, especially if they are difficult for them to perform.

We should always try to do those things that will earn us the prayers of our parents.

## WE HAVE LEARNED:

* As Muslims, we must worship Allah (SWT) alone.
* We must always be kind to our parents.
* We must show even humility and greater respect them when they grow old.

## DO WE KNOW THESE WORDS?

command
gracious word
contempt
to talk back
rebuke

# Section II

# Righteous Actions

Lesson 8

# The Losers and the Winners

بِسۡمِ ٱللَّهِ ٱلرَّحۡمَٰنِ ٱلرَّحِيمِ

وَٱلۡعَصۡرِ ١ إِنَّ ٱلۡإِنسَٰنَ لَفِي خُسۡرٍ

٢ إِلَّا ٱلَّذِينَ ءَامَنُواْ وَعَمِلُواْ ٱلصَّٰلِحَٰتِ

وَتَوَاصَوۡاْ بِٱلۡحَقِّ وَتَوَاصَوۡاْ بِٱلصَّبۡرِ ٣

*Wa-(a)l-'Aṣr(i). 'Inna-(a)l-' insāna lafī khusr(in).*
*'Illa-(a)lladhīna 'āmanū wa 'amilu-(a)ṣ-ṣaliḥāti*
*Wa-tawāṣaw bi-(a)l-ḥaqqi wa-tawāṣau bi-(a)ṣ-ṣabr(i)*

By the Time. Indeed! Human surely is in a loss.
Except those who believe, and do good works,
and mutually enjoin truth and mutually enjoin patience.
*('Al-'Aṣr 103-1-3)*

EXPLANATION:

In this short *Sūrah,* Allah (SWT) takes an oath of the Time *('Al-'Aṣr).* The Time is a witness to all human history. It has seen rise and fall of empires and kingdoms. It has seen powerful people come and go. It has seen cities, palaces, citadels built and destroyed.

The passage of the Time has also seen that human beings have been losing. Every day brings us closer to our death. No matter how much we may progress, we have no control over our lives and our future. Everything in this life is uncertain except the coming of death.

When death overtakes us, we leave everything behind. All of our money, property, family, friends, and power will be of no help when death arrives. No matter how much we may love a person, at the time of death we must part company and say good-bye. The only thing that will help us after our death is our faith and good deeds.

The Qur'ān reminds us that everyone in this life is a loser except the people who have the following four characteristics:

- those who have the right beliefs,
- those who act righteously,
- those who strive to establish the Truth,
- and those who strive to remain patient in difficulties.

These are, in fact, the characteristics of true Believers. It is important that our beliefs and actions are righteous. Both the right actions and the right beliefs are important in Islam.

A Believer must invite others to the truth of Islam. He must do so regularly. If he suffers any hardship while working for the cause of Islam, he must show patience. If something bad happens to him in personal life, he must turn to Allah (SWT) and ask His help.

Those who possess these characteristics are not the losers.They are successful ones, and their success is in both this world and in the Hereafter.

## True Religion

Rasūlullāh (S) advised us:

Allah (SWT) has fixed for everyone his right. Allah (SWT) has made some duties obligatory, and has declared certain things *Ḥalāl* and certain things *Harām*. He has chosen for you the religion which is easy, comforting, open and without narrowness.

*(At-Targhib wa-(a)t-Tarhīb)*

## WE HAVE LEARNED:

* The time has been a witness to the fact that all human beings are losers, except for those who believe.
* A true believer is an exception.
* He is successful in this life as well in the Hereafter.

## DO WE KNOW THESE WORDS?

*Al-'Asr*
characterstics
citadels
the Time
witness

Lesson 9

# Being a Muslim

بِسْمِ اللَّهِ الرَّحْمَٰنِ الرَّحِيمِ

لَا شَرِيكَ لَهُۥ وَبِذَٰلِكَ أُمِرْتُ
وَأَنَا۠ أَوَّلُ ٱلْمُسْلِمِينَ

*Lā sharīka la-hū wa-bi-dhālika 'umritu*
*wa-'anā 'awwalu-(a)l-Muslimīn*

No partners has He (Allah); I am commanded
to obey Him, and I am the first of the Muslims.
*('Al-'An'ām 6:163)*

EXPLANATION:

A Muslim is one who has accepted Islam. He worships Allah (SWT) alone and accepts no partners with Him. A Muslim knows that there is no power besides Allah (SWT) and he obeys His commands. A Muslim follows the righteous actions and avoids the wrong actions. The life of a Muslim must show us Islamic *'Akhlāq* in action.

Any act of a Muslim is done only for the sake of Allah (SWT). His *Ṣalāh* (prayer), his *Ṣawm* (fasting) and his sacrifices are for Allah (SWT). He lives to please Allah (SWT) and fulfill His Commands and he is ready to die for His sake. The complete life of a Muslim is fashioned according to Islamic *'Akhlāq.*

A Muslim knows Allah (SWT) is One and that He is our Creator and Lord. He worships none other than Him. He believes all human beings are created by Allah (SWT). He knows all creation belongs to Allah (SWT). He respects the rights of all human beings and all creations of Allah (SWT).

A true Muslim lives only by the teachings of the Qur'ān and the *Sunnah,* the way of Rasūlullāh (S). He always does the things that are *Ḥalāl* and he does not do the things that are *Ḥarām.* He practices what is right and avoids what is wrong.

A sincere Muslim invites everyone to Islam. If they accept the religion, he welcomes them as his brothers or sisters. If they reject Islam, he does not force them into accepting it. Instead, he prays that Allah (SWT) will help them see the light of

Islam. Allah (SWT) does not want us to use force in religion. A Muslim always sets a good example by practicing the teachings of Islam.

Islam means submission to Allah's Will. A Muslim is one who follows Islamic *'Akhlāq* with everyone and treats all human beings as one family of Allah (SWT).

We are Muslims and Allah (SWT) is our Lord and Creator. We follow Islamic *'Akhlāq* with all human beings and all creations of Allah.

In this book we shall read about those actions that we, as Muslims, must practice or avoid.

## Guidance of Allah (SWT)

فَمَن يُرِدِ ٱللَّهُ أَن يَهْدِيَهُۥ يَشْرَحْ صَدْرَهُۥ لِلْإِسْلَٰمِ
وَمَن يُرِدْ أَن يُضِلَّهُۥ يَجْعَلْ صَدْرَهُۥ ضَيِّقًا حَرَجًا
كَأَنَّمَا يَصَّعَّدُ فِى ٱلسَّمَآءِ كَذَٰلِكَ
يَجْعَلُ ٱللَّهُ ٱلرِّجْسَ عَلَى ٱلَّذِينَ لَا يُؤْمِنُونَ

Those whom Allah wills to guide, He opens their hearts to Islam. Whom He wills to leave straying, He makes their hearts closed and constricted, as if they had to climb up to the skies. Thus, Allah places impurity on those who refuse to believe.
*('Al-'An'ām 6:125)*

## WE HAVE LEARNED:

* A Muslim is one who worships Allah (SWT) alone.
* A Muslim follows the code of *Islamic 'Akhlāq* with everyone.
* A Muslim must set the best example of Islam in practice.

## DO WE KNOW THESE WORDS?

aspect
Guidance
*Ḥalāl*
*Ḥarām*
sacrifice
submission

Lesson 10

# Islamic Greetings

بِسْمِ اللَّهِ الرَّحْمَٰنِ الرَّحِيمِ

وَإِذَا جَاءَكَ الَّذِينَ يُؤْمِنُونَ بِآيَاتِنَا
فَقُلْ سَلَامٌ عَلَيْكُمْ

*Wa-'idha jā'aka-(a)lladhīna yu'minūna bi-'āyā ti-nā*
*fa-qul salāmun 'alai-kum*

When those come to you who believe in Our Signs,
greet them with *As-salāmu 'Alaikum,*
"May the peace of Allah be upon you."
*('Al-'An'ām 6:54)*

EXPLANATION:

A kind greeting shows our appreciation of others and our good wishes for them. Every group of people has a distinctive way of greeting others. The Qur'an teaches us a very unique greeting.

A Muslim greets another Muslim by saying, *"'As-salāmu 'Alai-kum."* This means: "May the Peace (of Allah) be upon you." The Islamic greeting is a *du'ā'*, prayer, from one Muslim to another.

The Muslim who is greeted responds with *"Wa-'Alaikum As-Salām,"* which means, "And upon you, may there be Peace as well." Thus, a Muslim who receives a *du'ā'* from a fellow Muslim returns it with a *du'ā'*. Both wish Peace and the Blessings of Allah (SWT) upon the other. The Qur'ān also teaches us:

وَإِذَا حُيِّيتُم بِتَحِيَّةٍ فَحَيُّوا بِأَحْسَنَ مِنْهَا أَوْ رُدُّوهَا

When a courteous greeting is offered to you,
you meet it with a greeting still more courteous,
or (at least) of equal courtesy.
*('An-Nisā' 4:86)*

The Qur'ān tells us that we must be even more courteous when responding to a greeting. To respond with *Wa-'Alai-kum As-Sālām* when we are greeted is the least that we can do. We may always add nice words of *du'ā'* to it.

For example, we may respond to *As-Salāmu 'Alai-kum* with *Wa-'Alai- kum As-Salāmu wa-Raḥmatu-(A)llāh,* which means, "May the Peace and Mercy of Allah (SWT) be upon you."

Sometimes people greet us with, *"As-Salāmu 'Alai-kum wa-Raḥmatu-(A)llāh."* We should answer them with something better. We must respond to them with, *"Wa-'Alai-kum As-Salāmu wa-Raḥmatu-(A)llāhi wa-Barakātu-hū,"* which means, "May the Peace, Mercy and Blessings of Allah be upon you."

Thus, when Muslims meet other Muslims, they not only greet them with nice words, but they also invite Allah's (SWT) Blessings and Mercy upon them.

When we meet non-Muslims, we must always be courteous to them. We must greet them with the best greetings that they use and understand. We must also respond to their greetings with beautiful and kind greetings.

## A Better Muslim

Rasūlullāh (S) said:
"It is not permissible for one Muslim
to keep his relations severed
with a brother for more
than three days.
Better among them is
one who is first to greet the other
with *'As-salāmu 'Alai-kum."*

*('Al-Bukhāri, Muslim)*

## WE HAVE LEARNED:

* The greeting of Islam is *'As-salāmu 'Alai-kum.*
* We must respond to the Islamic greeting with a similar, or even a better, one.
* We must greet everyone with the best greetings that they understand.

## DO WE KNOW THESE WORDS?

*'As-Salāmu 'Alai-kum*
courtesy
distinctive way
greetings
respond
*Wa-'Alai-kum 'As-Salām*
*Wa-'Alai-kum 'As-Salām Wa Raḥmatu (A)llāhi Wa Barakātu-hū*

Lesson 11

# Kind Deeds

بِسْمِ اللّٰهِ الرَّحْمٰنِ الرَّحِيْمِ

وَأَحْسِن كَمَآ أَحْسَنَ ٱللَّهُ إِلَيْكَ

*Wa- 'aḥsin kamā 'aḥsan(a)-Allāhu 'ilai-ka*

Be kind, as Allah has been kind to you.
*('Al-Qaṣaṣ 28:77)*

EXPLANATION:

Allah (SWT) is Most-Kind and Most-Merciful. It is out of kindness that He has made us human beings. He has given us beautiful bodies. He has given us brains to think with.

It is not possible to count all the blessings that Allah (SWT) has given us. We must thank Him for His Kindness. The best way to thank Allah (SWT) is to be kind to others by treating them nicely and speaking to them in a polite way.

We must help those who are in need. We must never harm others with our words or actions. When we do a favor to anyone we must remember Allah's favors to us. Allah's favors to us are much more than our favors can ever be to others. We must help everyone without regard to color, race, language and religion.

We should not expect anything in return for our favors. A Believer's reward is with Allah (SWT), and Allah's Kindness is the greatest reward one could ever have.

Allah (SWT) is *Rabbu-(A)l-'Ālamīn,* the Lord of All the Worlds. Our Prophet (S) was sent to the entire world as *Raḥmatun li-(a)l-'Ālamīn,* a Mercy to Humankind. Following his example, Muslims must be kind and merciful to all human beings.

Rasūlullāh (S) said:

> "He who does not respect elders and show kindness to youngsters is not from us."
> *(Musnad 'Ahmad 'Ibn Hanbal)*

Islam teaches us the meaning of kindness. Islam teaches us that all human beings have a right over us. Our families, friends and neighbors, and the wayfarer, the needy and the stranger all deserve our kindness and care.

Islam also teaches us that all the creations of Allah (SWT) have a right over us. We must be kind to animals. We must not hurt them, or kill them unnecessarily. If we keep them as pets for pleasure or service, then we must take special care of them.

We must also take care of plants and other forms of life. To plant a tree and care for it is also considered a good deed in Islam. Rasūlullāh (S) advised us:

> "If you have a sapling for planting in your hand and you come to know the Day of Judgment is going to take place tomorrow, plant it" *(Musnad 'Ibn Ḥanbal, Al-'Adab al-Mufrad by 'Al-Bukhāri)*

We must also take care of our environment as Allah (SWT) has placed everything in our trust. Allah (SWT) has appointed us the *Khalīfah,* the vicegerent of this world. Allah (SWT), in His Kindness, has given us a clean environment, we must thank Him by taking care of everything He has given us.

## Kind Words

وَقُل لِّعِبَادِى
يَقُولُوا۟ ٱلَّتِى هِىَ أَحْسَنُ

And say to My servants that they should only say those things that are best....
*('Al-'Isrā' 17:53)*

## WE HAVE LEARNED:

* A Muslim must always be kind to others.
* The best way to thank Allah (SWT) is to be kind to others.
* We must speak kindly to others, show respect to elders be kind to animals, and take care of the environment.

## DO WE KNOW THESE WORDS?

Blessings
gratitude
*Khalīfah*
*Raḥmatun li-(a)l-'Ālamīn*
respect
vicegerent

# Lesson 12

# Forgiveness

بِسْمِ اللّٰهِ الرَّحْمٰنِ الرَّحِيْمِ

ٱلَّذِينَ يُنفِقُونَ فِى ٱلسَّرَّآءِ وَٱلضَّرَّآءِ
وَٱلْكَـٰظِمِينَ ٱلْغَيْظَ وَٱلْعَافِينَ عَنِ ٱلنَّاسِ
وَٱللَّهُ يُحِبُّ ٱلْمُحْسِنِينَ

*'Alladhīna yunfiqūna fi-(a)s-sarrā' i wa-(a)ḍ-ḍarrā' i*
*wa-(a)l-kāẓimīna-(a)l-ghaiẓa wa-l-'āfīna 'ani-(a)n-nās(i),*
*wa-(A)llāhu yuḥibbu-(a)l-muḥsinīn.*

Those who spend (generously) in ease
and in difficulty, and those who control their anger,
and are forgiving towards people:
Surely, Allah loves those who do good.
*('Al 'Imrān 3:134)*

From this verse, we learn two very important things. One is to spend money in the way of Allah (SWT). The other is to control our anger and to forgive others. The first point has already been discussed in Lesson 11. Here we shall explain the second point.

Controlling anger and forgiving others are two qualities that are related to each other. In moments of anger we lose control over ourselves. We may say or do things that we may later regret. By controlling our anger, we can think clearly and reasonably.

Rasūlullāh (S) advised us not to lose our tempers, saying that if we become really angry we should sit down. If we cannot control ourselves even then, we must lie down. *(Mishkāt)*

Forgiveness is a very important virtue in Islam. If we are in a position to take revenge and, instead, we choose to forgive, Allah (SWT) becomes pleased with us. Additionally, forgiveness may create a good feeling in the heart of the person we forgive, and he may become a friend. However, we do not have to forgive someone if we choose not to. It is our right to retaliate, but it is our privilege to forgive.

Allah (SWT) says in the Qur'ān:

وَجَزَٰٓؤُا۟ سَيِّئَةٍ سَيِّئَةٌ مِّثْلُهَا ۖ فَمَنْ عَفَا وَأَصْلَحَ

فَأَجْرُهُۥ عَلَى ٱللَّهِ ۚ إِنَّهُۥ لَا يُحِبُّ ٱلظَّٰلِمِينَ

An evil could be returned with equal punishment;
but he that forgives and makes peace,
his reward is due from Allah: Indeed! He
(Allah) does not love those who do injustice.
*('Ash-Shūrā 42:40)*

One is morally right in demanding retaliation against someone who has wronged him. It is an injustice to refuse the right of retaliation to one who has been wronged. Often, powerful and influential people commit injustices against those who are weaker. If the weak are not given the right to retaliate, there will be injustice and oppression in society.

When taking retaliation, one should not take the law into his own hands. Instead, one should approach the police and the courts of law. Taking the law into one's hands may result in bloodshed and further injustice.

Forgiveness, instead of retaliation, is a good act, especially in the case of one's own family. When some members of one's family misbehave and show enmity, the Qur'ān advises us to show special kindness:

يَٰٓأَيُّهَا ٱلَّذِينَ ءَامَنُوٓا۟ إِنَّ مِنْ أَزْوَٰجِكُمْ وَأَوْلَٰدِكُمْ

عَدُوًّا لَّكُمْ فَٱحْذَرُوهُمْ ۚ وَإِن تَعْفُوا۟ وَتَصْفَحُوا۟ وَتَغْفِرُوا۟

فَإِنَّ ٱللَّهَ غَفُورٌ رَّحِيمٌ

O you who believe! Truly among your wives
and your children are (some that are) enemies
to yourself: So beware of them!
But if you forgive, overlook and cover up
(their faults) Indeed! Allah is
Oft-forgiving, Most-Merciful.
*('At-Taghābun 64:14)*

## WE HAVE LEARNED:

* Charity and forgiveness are two of the most important virtues in Islam.
* A person who has been wronged has the right to retaliate in Islam, but forgiveness is more loved by Allah (SWT).
* We must be most generous and most forgiving to our family.

## DO WE KNOW THESE WORDS?

injustice
oppression
recommend
retaliate
virtue, virtuous
wronged

Lesson 13

# Show Patience

بِسْمِ اللّٰهِ الرَّحْمٰنِ الرَّحِيْمِ

يَٰٓأَيُّهَا ٱلَّذِينَ ءَامَنُوا۟ ٱصْبِرُوا۟ وَصَابِرُوا۟ وَرَابِطُوا۟

*Ya 'ayyuha-(a)lladhīna 'āmanū (i)ṣbirū wa-ṣābirū wa- rābitū*

Oh Believers, show patience and be better than others in patience, and support each other to do right.
*('Al 'Imrān 3:200)*

EXPLANATION:

A Believer must always be thankful when his life is easy and patient when he is faced with difficulties. If we are patient and turn to Allah (SWT) in our difficulties, He helps us. We should keep our faith in Him at all times.

A Believer should be more patient than others. He must be an example of one who has faith in Allah's Mercy. Ease and difficulty in our lives are both tests from Allah (SWT).

Muslims are brothers and sisters to each other. We must support each other during times of ease and hardship. This support may be in the form of our contribution in money or time and effort. Even our few words of sympathy during times of difficulty are of great help to those who are in difficulty.

Prophet Muhammad (S) said:

> "Support your Muslim brother both when someone is doing wrong to him, as well as when he is doing wrong to someone."

His *Ṣaḥābah* asked him:

> "O Messenger, we can support him when someone is doing wrong to him, but how can we support him when he is doing wrong to someone?"

Rasūlullāh (S) replied:

> "By stopping him from his doing wrong to someone."
> *('Al-Bukhārī and Muslim)*

Muslims must only support each other in doing those things

which are right. We must not support each other in doing wrong things.

If any Muslim does anything wrong, other Muslims must stop him. The true friendship is not to support our brothers and sisters when they do wrong but helping them to always do the right things.

We must remember that Islam teaches us to be just with everyone. Islam enjoins upon us to help everyone in need. As Muslims, we must work together for the good of all. Muslims have special rights over each other.

Muslims, as individuals, as families and as members of the human society, must always strive to do the right, to be patient in difficulties and to support those who need our help.

## Six Rights of Muslims

Rasūlullāh (S) advised us :
"Every Muslim has six rights
over other Muslims:
• When you meet a Muslim,
say, '*Assalamu 'Alaikum*
• When he invites you, accept his invitation
• When he needs your advice, offer it
• When he sneezes and says *Alḥamdu li-Allāh* (All Praises are due to Allah),
answer him with *Yarḥamu-ka-Allāh*
(May Allah have Mercy upon you)
•When he falls sick, offer consolation
•When he dies, participate in the funeral.

*(Muslim)*

## WE HAVE LEARNED:

* A Believer must always place his trust in Allah (SWT) and be patient.

* Muslims must always support each other to do right.

* Muslims must stop other Muslims from doing wrong.

## DO WE KNOW THESE WORDS?

contribution
doing right
doing wrong
hardships
patience
sympathetic

Lesson

# 14

# Justice

بِسْمِ ٱللَّهِ ٱلرَّحْمَٰنِ ٱلرَّحِيمِ

يَٰٓأَيُّهَا ٱلَّذِينَ ءَامَنُوا۟ كُونُوا۟ قَوَّٰمِينَ لِلَّهِ
شُهَدَآءَ بِٱلْقِسْطِ ۖ وَلَا يَجْرِمَنَّكُمْ شَنَـَٔانُ
قَوْمٍ عَلَىٰٓ أَلَّا تَعْدِلُوا۟ ۚ ٱعْدِلُوا۟ هُوَ أَقْرَبُ لِلتَّقْوَىٰ ۖ
وَٱتَّقُوا۟ ٱللَّهَ ۚ إِنَّ ٱللَّهَ خَبِيرٌۢ بِمَا تَعْمَلُونَ

*Yā 'ayyuha-(a)lladhīna 'āmanu kūnū qawwāmina li-(A)llāhi shuhadā'a bi-(a)l-qist, wa-lā yajrimanna-kum shana'ānu qawmin 'alā 'al-lā ta'dilū, 'i'dilū huwa 'aqrabu li-(a)t-taqwā, wa-(a)t-taqū Allāh(a)', 'inna-Allaha Khabīrun bi-mā ta'malūn.*

Oh you who believe! Stand out firmly as witnesses
to Allah in fair dealing. And let not the hatred of
others to you make you swerve from justice.
Be just: that is next to piety, and fear Allah.
Allah is Well-Informed of what you do.
*('Al-Mā'idah 5:8)*

EXPLANATION:

Islam teaches in fairness and justice for all. Every Muslim must be fair and just. The Islamic *'Ummah* has been created by Allah (SWT) as justly balanced.

وَكَذَٰلِكَ جَعَلْنَٰكُمْ أُمَّةً وَسَطًا لِّتَكُونُوا۟
شُهَدَآءَ عَلَى ٱلنَّاسِ وَيَكُونَ ٱلرَّسُولُ عَلَيْكُمْ شَهِيدًا ۗ

Thus, We have made out of you a justly balanced
*'Ummah* that you might be witness over the nations,
and the Messenger be a witness over you.
*('Al-Baqarah 2:143)*

The Qur'ān uses two words for justice; *qist* and *'adl*. Both have meaning of "fairness and justice." We must not have prejudices against any individual or community. We should not put wrong meanings to another person's words. We should not doubt the motives behind any person's actions.

Justice means that we must have the same set of standards and rules for everyone. We should treat everyone fairly. If we have to judge between two parties, we should be just.

In general, people give up fairness and justice for two reasons: one is the hatred of an individual or a group of people, and the other is the love for some person or group of people. No matter how much we may dislike a person, group or community, Islam wants us to be fair and just to all people, even to our enemies.

Islam also wants us to be fair and just when our own interests are involved. We must stand for justice and the truth, even if sometimes we have to stand against our relatives, friends, community, nation or ourselves.

Some people believe that their people or their nation can never be wrong. Islam does not support this idea. The Qur'ān teaches us:

فَاعْدِلُوا وَلَوْ كَانَ ذَا قُرْبَىٰ ۖ وَبِعَهْدِ اللَّهِ أَوْفُوا ۚ
ذَٰلِكُمْ وَصَّاكُم بِهِ لَعَلَّكُمْ تَذَكَّرُونَ

Speak for justice even if it goes against
your relative. Be true to the covenant
of Allah, this He commands you,
so that you may remember.
*('Al-'An'ām 6:152)*

To practice fairness and justice is an act of piety which shows our love of Allah (SWT) and His Messengers.

## WE HAVE LEARNED:

* A Muslim must be just and fair all the time.
* Neither the enemity of our enemies nor the love of our friends and relatives should distract us from justice.
* Muslim *'Ummah* is a justly balanced *'Ummah* and it works for the common justice to all.

## DO WE KNOW THESE WORDS?

*'adl*
balanced
covenant
*qist*
justice
equality

# Lesson 15

# Fulfill Promises

بِسۡمِ ٱللَّهِ ٱلرَّحۡمَٰنِ ٱلرَّحِيمِ

يَٰٓأَيُّهَا ٱلَّذِينَ ءَامَنُوٓاْ أَوۡفُواْ بِٱلۡعُقُودِۚ

*Ya 'ayyuha (a)lladhīna 'āmanū 'awfū bi-(a)l-'uqūd(i). . .*

Oh Believers, fulfill your promises. . .
*('Al-Mā'idah 5:1)*

EXPLANATION:

Allah (SWT) wants Muslims to be fair and just in all their dealings and fulfill their promises. Muslims must be fair and fulfill their promises not only to fellow Muslims but also to all people. In life we make many commitments and promises. Some of them are legal in nature, and we often write them down. These types of promises are called agreements, contracts or covenants. Breaking such promises often results in punishment by the courts of law.

Most of our promises are, however, oral, and not written. We make such promises every day to our family, friends, neighbors and colleagues. All the promises written and unwritten are very serious commitments and must be fulfilled. By breaking them, we break a very important rule of living together. We are not only responsible to the person to whom we make the promise, but to Allah (SWT), Himself.

The Qur'ān says:

وَأَوۡفُواْ بِٱلۡعَهۡدِۖ إِنَّ ٱلۡعَهۡدَ كَانَ مَسۡـُٔولٗا

> And fulfill promise, for about every promise it will be asked (on the Day of Judgment).
> *(Banī 'Isrā'il 17:34)*

Every promise we make, we accept Allah (SWT) as our witness. It is Allah (SWT) who will ask us about our unfulfilled promises.

We have also made a promise to Allah (SWT), before our descent on Earth. Allah (SWT) asked us: "Am I your Lord?" and we answered Him, " Yes, of course You are our Lord!"

Allah (SWT) reminds us of that promise in the Qur'ān and promises us:

وَأَوْفُواْ بِعَهْدِىٓ أُوفِ بِعَهْدِكُمْ

And you shall fulfill your promise
and I shall fulfill My Promise.
*('Al-Baqarah 2:40)*

And Allah (SWT) loves those who fulfill their promises:

بَلَىٰ مَنْ أَوْفَىٰ بِعَهْدِهِۦ
وَٱتَّقَىٰ فَإِنَّ ٱللَّهَ يُحِبُّ ٱلْمُتَّقِينَ

Yes! (The chosen of Allah is he) who fulfills his promise and fears Allah. For Allah loves those who fear Him.
*('Al 'Imrān 3:76)*

But there are people who do not care about their promises and for one reason or another, they break their promises with Allah (SWT); Allah (SWT) promises great punishment for them:

إِنَّ ٱلَّذِينَ يَشْتَرُونَ بِعَهْدِ ٱللَّهِ وَأَيْمَـٰنِهِمْ ثَمَنًا قَلِيلًا
أُوْلَـٰٓئِكَ لَا خَلَـٰقَ لَهُمْ فِى ٱلْـَٔاخِرَةِ

Indeed! Those who buy a small gain at the cost of Allah's Covenant and their oaths (firm promises), they will have no portion in the Hereafter.
*('Al 'Imrān 3:77)*

Allah (SWT) says in the Qur'ān about the Believers:

وَٱلَّذِينَ هُمْ لِأَمَـٰنَـٰتِهِمْ وَعَهْدِهِمْ رَٰعُونَ

(The Believers) are those who keep their trust and fulfill their promises.
*('Al-Mu'minūn 23:8)*

## WE HAVE LEARNED:

* A Muslim must always fulfill his promise.
* If we shall fulfill our promises, Allah (SWT) will fulfill His Promises to us.
* Those who break their promises with Allah (SWT) will have no share in the *'Ākhīrah.*

## DO WE KNOW THESE WORDS?

agreements
commitment
contracts
covenant
decent
profit

Lesson 16

# Just Measure

بِسْمِ اللَّهِ الرَّحْمَٰنِ الرَّحِيمِ

أَوْفُوا الْكَيْلَ وَلَا تَكُونُوا مِنَ الْمُخْسِرِينَ ﴿١٨١﴾
وَزِنُوا بِالْقِسْطَاسِ الْمُسْتَقِيمِ ﴿١٨٢﴾
وَلَا تَبْخَسُوا النَّاسَ أَشْيَاءَهُمْ
وَلَا تَعْثَوْا فِي الْأَرْضِ مُفْسِدِينَ ﴿١٨٣﴾

*'Awfū-(a)l-kaila wa-la-takūnū mina (a)l-mukhsirīn(a)*
*Wazinū bi-(a)l-qisṭāsi (a)l-mustaqīm.*
*Wa-lā tabkhasu-(a)n-nāsa 'ashyā 'a-hum,*
*wa-lā ta'thaw fi-(a)l-'arḍi mufsidīn.*

Give just measure, and cause no loss
(to others by cheating). Weigh with scales true
and upright. And withhold not things due to people,
and do not spread mischief in the land.
*('Ash-Shu'arā' 26: 181-183)*

EXPLANATION:

A Muslim must always be honest and just. A Muslim must always be responsible and fair. Allah (SWT) wants Muslim businessmen to always be fair and honest with all people.

The Qur'ān advises us again and again:

وَيَٰقَوْمِ أَوْفُوا الْمِكْيَالَ وَالْمِيزَانَ بِالْقِسْطِ ۖ
وَلَا تَبْخَسُوا النَّاسَ أَشْيَاءَهُمْ وَلَا تَعْثَوْا فِي الْأَرْضِ مُفْسِدِينَ

Oh my people! Give full measure and just weight
and do not withhold from people things which are theirs.
And do not make evil in the land, causing mischief.
*(Hūd 11:85)*

Some people want to make more money, and they do it by cheating other people. They deliver less than what they promise. They make false claims which they do not fulfill. They do not keep their word after a deal has been made.

Their desire to make more and more money makes them deceive others.

There is no doubt that sometimes more money can be made by being dishonest than by being honest. But the profits which come as a result of unfair practices are only in the short run. When customers discover that they have been cheated by someone, they lose respect for that person. People do not want to do business with him anymore.

They may tell others not to deal with that person and as a result, the cheater will lose even more money because of his dishonesty. When the government finds out, he may even be arrested and punished.

The most important thing that the dishonest person loses, however, is the *Barakah* (blessings) from Allah (SWT), given to those who make an honest living. The punishment in this world is only the beginning of what awaits them in the Hereafter. Thus, they suffer for their dishonesty both in this world and in the next.

Rasūlullāh (S) has told us always to eat what is *Ḥalāl* (permissible)and *Ṭayyib* (pure). Only *Ḥalāl* and *Ṭayyib* things are allowed in Islam. Ḥalāl things are not only those that are pure in themselves but they are those which are earned in the right way.

When people become dishonest and greedy, they spread mischief in the world. People start losing trust in each other.

Muslims must always measure justly, be fair in all dealings and keep up their promises and agreements.

## WE HAVE LEARNED:

* Allah (SWT) wants a Muslim to be always just and honest in his dealings with other people.
* Only *Ḥalāl* and *Ṭayyib* earnings are permitted in Islam.
* Dishonesty and injustice spread mischief and destroy the peacefulness of the society.

## DO WE KNOW THESE WORDS?

*barakah*
dealing
deceive
*Ḥalāl*
*Ṭayyib*
unfair practice
upright

# Lesson 17

# The Trust

بِسۡمِ ٱللَّهِ ٱلرَّحۡمَٰنِ ٱلرَّحِيمِ

إِنَّ ٱللَّهَ يَأۡمُرُكُمۡ أَن تُؤَدُّواْ ٱلۡأَمَٰنَٰتِ
إِلَىٰٓ أَهۡلِهَا وَإِذَا حَكَمۡتُم بَيۡنَ ٱلنَّاسِ أَن تَحۡكُمُواْ
بِٱلۡعَدۡلِۚ إِنَّ ٱللَّهَ نِعِمَّا يَعِظُكُم بِهِۦٓۗ
إِنَّ ٱللَّهَ كَانَ سَمِيعَۢا بَصِيرٗا

*'Inn(a) Allāha ya'muru-kum 'an tu'addū-(a)l-'amānāti*
*'ilā 'ahli-hā wa-'idhā ḥakam-tum baina-(a)n-nāsi 'an taḥkumū*
*bi-(a)l-'adl(i): 'inna-Allāha ni'imma-ya'iẓu-kum bi-hī,*
*'inna-Allāha kāna Samī'an Baṣīrā*

Indeed! Allah commands you to give back the trusts
(deposits) to their owners; and when you judge among
people, judge with justice:
Verily how excellent is the teaching He gives you;
for Allah is He Who hears and sees everything.
*('An-Nisā' 4:58)*

EXPLANATION:

To trust one another is very important in society. Family, friends and neighbors must have mutual trust and the desire to help one another in times of need. Sometimes we must leave our children, valuables, and possessions as a trust *('amānah)* in the care of others. Similarly, we must do the same for others when they need us.

The trust *('al-'amānah)* is to honestly safeguard whatever has been put in our care. Whenever we are asked to return the *'amānah* (the entrusted thing) to its rightful owner, we must return it promptly and without hesitation. We must return the *'amānah* in the same condition as we received it.

A trust is also a kind of promise or agreement. It is a promise to take good care of the *'amānah* and return it when it is asked for. Using the *'amānah,* or not returning it, is called the *khiyānah.* The *khiyānah* means breaking the trust.

Allah (SWT) advises us in the Qur'ān:

يَٰٓأَيُّهَا ٱلَّذِينَ ءَامَنُوا۟ لَا تَخُونُوا۟ ٱللَّهَ وَٱلرَّسُولَ وَتَخُونُوٓا۟ أَمَٰنَٰتِكُمْ وَأَنتُمْ تَعْلَمُونَ

Oh Believers! betray not the trust of
Allah and His Messenger,
nor knowingly betray your trust.
*('Al-'Anfāl 8:27)*

Betraying the trust of Allah (SWT) and His Messenger means not to follow the teachings of the Qur'ān and the *Sunnah* of Rasūlullāh (S).

Allah (SWT) has given this world as an *'amānah* to human beings. To worship Allah (SWT) alone, follow His Laws, and take good care of our society and environment.

To keep one's trust with human beings is also to keep one's trust with Allah (SWT) and His Messenger (S). To break a moral law is to break one's trust with Allah (SWT).

Keeping a secret for someone is also a trust. The sharing of such secret information with others is the *khiyānah*. To give advice to someone is also a trust. A person who seeks our advice trusts our opinion and we must offer him the best advice and in full confidence.

Many people deceive and betray their trust to get more money for their families. The *ḥarām* earnings do not bring comfort to the family. Rather, they bring Allah's (SWT) anger upon them; and in the end, they are the losers.

The Qur'ān promises that the Believers "who faithfully observe their trusts and their covenants" *('Al-Mu'minūn 23:1-8)* will be successful and attain Paradise.

## WE HAVE LEARNED:

* A Believer must always keep the trust.
* When the owner demands his *'amānah*, we must return it promptly.
* To do *khiyānah* with an *'amānah* is a great sin in the Sight of Allah (SWT).

## DO WE KNOW THESE WORDS?

covenant
the *'amānah*
in confidence
the *khiyānah*

Lesson 18

# The Middle Path

بِسْمِ اللَّهِ الرَّحْمَٰنِ الرَّحِيمِ

وَلَا تَجْعَلْ يَدَكَ مَغْلُولَةً إِلَىٰ عُنُقِكَ
وَلَا تَبْسُطْهَا كُلَّ الْبَسْطِ
فَتَقْعُدَ مَلُومًا مَّحْسُورًا

*Wa- lā taj'al yada-ka maghlūlatan 'ilā 'unuqi-ka*
*wa-lā tabsuṭ-hā kulla-(a)l-basti*
*fa-taq'uda malūman maḥṣūrā*

Make not your hand tied to your neck,
nor open it with a complete opening,
so that you are blamed and become regretful.
*('Al-'Isrā' 17:29)*

EXPLANATION:

Moderation means to avoid doing too much or too little of something. Islam teaches us to practice moderation in everything we do. Islam wants us to do those things that need to be done in a decent manner.

Some religions teach that we can only gain the pleasure of God if we give up everything that we love. They teach, the more we suffer in this life, the greater will be the rewards in the afterlife. The people who follow such religions give up their families, properties and worldly comforts and they voluntarily suffer hardship.

There are other people who claim that we should enjoy our lives as much as possible since there is no life after death. They teach that we should concern ourselves with our own pleasures and should not worry about anyone else.

Islam teaches us that the best way to lead our lives is by doing all things in moderation. To enjoy the blessings that Allah (SWT) has given us is to show our thanks and use them in moderation. To share the blessings of Allah (SWT) with others is also a way of showing our gratefulness to Him.

Some people are stingy and miserly. They have money but they do not want to spend it. They do not contribute to charities. If a needy person comes to them, they rebuke him and turn him away. Other people waste their money and spend it on things that they really do not need. They are easily tired of the things they have and always desire more and more.

Both kinds of people are disliked by Allah (SWT). We should live moderately, spending our money properly on ourselves, on the needy and on charities. We should thank Allah (SWT) for having blessed us with it.

We must share our wealth with our families, relatives, the needy and any good cause which helps the society. We must trust in Allah (SWT) and do things as He commands us to. Our generosity to others does not decrease our wealth but rather, it adds to the *Barakah* of our lives.

## Allah's Blessings

Allah (SWT) reminds Rasūlullāh (S) of His favors and advises him:

فَأَمَّا ٱلْيَتِيمَ فَلَا تَقْهَرْ وَأَمَّا ٱلسَّآئِلَ فَلَا تَنْهَرْ

وَأَمَّا بِنِعْمَةِ رَبِّكَ فَحَدِّثْ

"So, oppress not the orphan and do not rebuke a beggar and speak of the blessings of your Lord."

*(Aḍ-Ḍuḥā 93:9-11)*

## WE HAVE LEARNED:

* We should not be wasteful in spending our money.
* We should not be miserly by hoarding our wealth.
* Islam teaches us the path of moderation.

## DO WE KNOW THESE WORDS?

*Al-Barakah*
moderation
miserly
rebuke

Lesson 19

# Sadaqah: Charity

بِسۡمِ ٱللَّهِ ٱلرَّحۡمَٰنِ ٱلرَّحِيمِ

مَّثَلُ ٱلَّذِينَ يُنفِقُونَ أَمۡوَٰلَهُمۡ
فِي سَبِيلِ ٱللَّهِ كَمَثَلِ حَبَّةٍ أَنۢبَتَتۡ سَبۡعَ
سَنَابِلَ فِي كُلِّ سُنۢبُلَةٖ مِّاْئَةُ حَبَّةٖۗ وَٱللَّهُ
يُضَٰعِفُ لِمَن يَشَآءُۚ وَٱللَّهُ وَٰسِعٌ عَلِيمٌ

*Mat͟halu-(a)l-lad͟hīna yunfiqūna 'amwāla-hum fī sabīli—(A)llāhi ka-mat͟hali ḥabbatin 'anbatat sab'a sanā-bila fī kulli sunbulatin mi'atu ḥabbah(tin), wa-(A)llāhu yuḍā'ifu li-man yas͟hā'u, wa-(A)llāhu Wāsi'un 'Alīm(un)*

The example of those who spend their wealth
in the way of Allah is that of a corn: it grows
seven ears, and each ear has a hundred grains.
Allah gives manifold increase to whom He pleases:
And Allah cares for all and He knows all things.
*('Al-Baqarah 2: 261)*

EXPLANATION:

The Qur'ān teaches us to be kind and generous towards others. Some people have been blessed with more wealth than they will ever need. There are others who do not even have enough to support themselves and their families. It is the duty of those who have more to share with those who have less.

The blessings of Allah (SWT) for charity cannot be measured in numbers. For our understanding Allah (SWT) is giving us an example of a seed of corn, which grows into a plant. The plant grows into seven ears and each ear has one hundred grains. Each act of charity brings us a reward of seven-hundred times and much more. Imagine then how Allah (SWT) rewards us when we do good deeds. In fact, there is no earthly limit to the Blessings of Allah (SWT) .

Giving in the way of Allah (SWT) brings *Barakah* into our lives. The more we give, the more *Barakah* we receive from Allah (SWT). Everything we spend to help others is returned to us many times over by Allah (SWT).

One way of spending in the way of Allah (SWT) is by giving our money to charities. We can also help building *Masājid,* schools, hospitals, orphanages, and homes for the homeless. We can also plant trees, dig wells, or build canals.

Such actions are called the *Ṣadaqah Jāriyah.* The *Ṣadaqah Jāriyah* is a charity which continues through time. So long as this charity continues, the *thawāb* (reward) we earn from it continues.

Spending in this world to help others is also the best saving we can have for the *'Ākhirah.* Thus, by helping others, we are actually helping ourselves.
The only condition that Allah (SWT) places on good deeds or acts of charity to obtain His Blessings is that we are sincere in our intentions. We must be charitable only to gain the pleasure of Allah (SWT). Any act which is performed to show off, or which is followed by injury or unkind words is not acceptable to Allah (SWT).

قَوْلٌ مَّعْرُوفٌ وَمَغْفِرَةٌ خَيْرٌ مِّن صَدَقَةٍ يَتْبَعُهَآ أَذًى وَٱللَّهُ غَنِىٌّ حَلِيمٌ

A kind word and forgiveness is better than
charity, followed by injury:
Allah is Self-Sufficient and Clement.
*('Al-Baqarah 2:263)*

## *Ṣadaqah Jāriyah*

"When a human dies, all his actions are cut off except the three; a continuous charity (*Ṣadaqah Jāriyah*) knowledge that benefits others and a child that remembers him in prayers and good deeds."
*(Muslim)*

## WE HAVE LEARNED:

* *Ṣadaqah* means to spend in the way of Allah (SWT).
* *Ṣadaqah* is a saving for the *'Ākhirah.*
* By helping others we, in fact, help ourselves.

## DO WE KNOW THESE WORDS?

charity
continuous
fortunate
generous
*Ṣadaqah Jāriyah*
*thawāb*

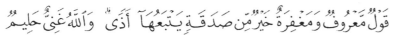

بِسْمِ اللَّهِ الرَّحْمَٰنِ الرَّحِيمِ

وَاقْصِدْ فِي مَشْيِكَ وَاغْضُضْ مِن صَوْتِكَ
إِنَّ أَنكَرَ الْأَصْوَاتِ لَصَوْتُ الْحَمِيرِ

*Wa-(a)qṣid fī ma<u>sh</u>yi-ka wa-(a)<u>gh</u>ḍud min ṣawti-ka*
*'inna 'ankara-(a)l-' aṣwāti la-ṣawtu-(a)l ḥamīr*

And be moderate in your walk and lower your voice,
Indeed! The loudest of all voices is the braying of an ass.
*(Luqmān 31:19)*

EXPLANATION:

Allah (SWT) loves those who are modest and humble. Modest people do not boast and they are not arrogant or proud. They treat others with respect. They do not create mischief or provoke others to do mischief.

Modest people are polite in their talk and gentle in their walk. In conversation, they do not raise their voices or use foul language. If they are in disgreement with others, they express themselves clearly and politely. When they speak, they do so in a mild language. They are always prepared to listen to other people's opinions.

Some people are excessively proud. They walk in an arrogant manner and when they speak, their tone is harsh. They do not realize that their physical power and beautiful appearance is a gift from Allah (SWT). One day, they will become old and weak. Death will surely overtake them and they will be held accoutable for their arrogance.

Many youth spend their energy by joining gangs and fighting others. The gangs spread much mischief and often spill much blood. They endanger their own lives and the lives of others. They disturb the peace of the society.

The braying of a donkey is very loud and unpleasant. When we shout in anger, we are following the braying of the donkey. In anger we may say things which may hurt others. When we are angry, we are under the control of the *<u>Sh</u>aiṭān,* whose purpose is to cause enmity and discord among people.

Conversation in a low voice and polite manner may be heard and understood better. People with good manners listen to others and are polite when they talk to them. They know that by shouting during an argument they will not accomplish anything. We can never convince anyone with an angry argument.

Allah (SWT) says:

وَقُل لِّعِبَادِي يَقُولُوا الَّتِي هِيَ أَحْسَنُ

إِنَّ الشَّيْطَانَ يَنزَغُ بَيْنَهُمْ

Tell my servants to say only those things that are best. For *Shaiṭān* does sow discord (enmity) between them.
*('Al-'Isrā' 17:53)*

As Muslims, we must overcome this weakness and try to be moderate in our walk and modest in our talk. We must inspire others to do the same by our pleasing manners of walk and pleasant speech.

## WE HAVE LEARNED:

* A believer should walk with humility and should speak politely.
* We cannot convince any one by shouting.
* If Muslims argue with others, they should do so in a decent manner.

## DO WE KNOW THESE WORDS?

argument
conversation
humility
arrogant
humble
pride

# Lesson 21

# Self-Sacrifice

بِسْمِ ٱللَّهِ ٱلرَّحْمَٰنِ ٱلرَّحِيمِ

وَيُؤْثِرُونَ عَلَىٰٓ أَنفُسِهِمْ
وَلَوْ كَانَ بِهِمْ خَصَاصَةٌ ۚ وَمَن يُوقَ شُحَّ
نَفْسِهِۦ فَأُو۟لَٰٓئِكَ هُمُ ٱلْمُفْلِحُونَ

*Wa- yu' thirūna 'alā ' anfusi-him*
*wa law kāna bi-him khaṣāṣah wa-man yūqa shuḥḥa*
*nafsi-hī fā-' ulā' ika humu-(a)l-mufliḥūn.*

And they prefer them (others) over their own selves,
though poverty was their lot. And whoever
is saved from the greed of one's own soul,
they are the ones who are successful.
*('Al-Ḥashr 59:9)*

EXPLANATION:

Islam teaches us self-sacrifice for the sake of Allah (SWT), for His Messenger (S) and for our fellow human beings. Allah (SWT) wants us to seek reward for this sacrifice from Him alone. In self-sacrifice, the intention of the Believer must be pure, and he should seek no reward, praise or return from anyone for his actions.

Islam teaches us to sacrifice and share whatever Allah (SWT) has blessed us with. As Muslims, we are obligated to give the *Zakāh* and the *Ṣadaqah* as acts of charity. In addition, we should give gifts of love and friendship to others. We must take care of our families, relatives, the needy and the orphans. We must give our time and effort for the cause of Islam. We should offer our expertise and wisdom to benefit others.

This verse of the Qur'ān describes the admirable characteristics of the *'Anṣār* of *Madīnah.* The *'Anṣār* have set a beautiful example for us to follow. When the *Muhājirūn* migrated from Makkah, they left all their possessions behind. The *'Anṣār* shared their money and property with their Muslim brothers, in spite of their own financial difficulties.

The *'Anṣār* did not want anything in return from the *Muḥājirūn* and only desired their reward from Allah (SWT). The *'Anṣār* of *Madīnah* have set the best example of self-sacrifice for all Believers to follow.

Self-sacrifice is not simply giving what we have an excess of. Self-sacrifice is sharing our belongings, even when we do not have enough for ourselves. Self-sacrifice is to give up our most valuable possessions for the sake of Allah (SWT), to help others. Self-sacrifice is giving our time to the cause of Islam, even when we are busy.

The Qur'ān reminds us:

لَن تَنَالُوا۟ ٱلْبِرَّ حَتَّىٰ تُنفِقُوا۟ مِمَّا تُحِبُّونَ

You shall not reach good
unless you spend that what you love.
*('Al 'Imrān 3: 92)*

A true test of our faith in Allah (SWT) is to give up those things that we love and desire for ourselves. We readily make sacrifices for our family and friends. The greater sacrifice is to do the same for those whom we do not even know or for a good cause. By doing so, we are rewarded by Allah (SWT) many times over.

## Helping Others

"Whoever feeds his hungry brother,
till his hunger is removed, and offered his
thirsty brother water till his thirst was
quenched, Allah will keep him from the
fire at a distance of seven ditches;
each ditch from the other is at a
five hundred year distance."
*(Aṭ-Ṭabarāni)*

## WE HAVE LEARNED:

* Self-sacrifice is more than giving our spare money and extra time for Islam and to service others.

* Self-sacrifice means sharing our possessions even when we do not have them in excess of our needs.

* Self-sacrifice is to help others by giving from those things that we love for the sake of Allah (SWT).

## DO WE KNOW THESE WORDS?

*'Anṣār*
*Muhājirūn*
self-sacrifice
*Ṣaḥābah*

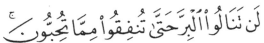

## Section III

# Wrong Actions

بِسْمِ اللهِ الرَّحْمٰنِ الرَّحِيْمِ

يَٰٓأَيُّهَا ٱلَّذِينَ ءَامَنُوٓا۟ إِنَّمَا ٱلْخَمْرُ
وَٱلْمَيْسِرُ وَٱلْأَنصَابُ وَٱلْأَزْلَٰمُ
رِجْسٌ مِّنْ عَمَلِ ٱلشَّيْطَٰنِ فَٱجْتَنِبُوهُ
لَعَلَّكُمْ تُفْلِحُونَ

*Yā 'ayyuha-(a)lladhīna 'āmanū 'innama-(a)l-khamru*
*wa-(a)l-maisiru wa-(a)l-'anṣābu wa-(a)l-'azlāmu*
*rijsun min 'amali-(a)sh-shaiṭāni fa-(a)jtanibū-hu*
*la 'alla-kum tufliḥūn*

Oh you who Believe! Indeed, the intoxicants,
the gambling, the idols and divining with arrows
are abomination of *Shaiṭān's* work, leave it aside,
that you may succeed.
*('Al-Mā'idah 5:90)*

EXPLANATION:

Allah (SWT) completely forbids four things which are the works of *Shaiṭān,* who is a known enemy of Humankind. The *Shaiṭān* wants to make us go astray from the right path of Islam.

The first of the forbidden things is *'Al-Khamr* (intoxicants, alcohol and drugs), which includes all those things that numb our senses. Our minds and bodies are gifts and trusts from Allah (SWT), therefore, we must safeguard them. Alcohol and drugs destroy our bodies and minds and can endanger the lives of others. Because they are addictive, people cannot easily give these bad habits up.

*'Al-Maisir,* the gambling, is another vice which destroys the individual and the society. Gambling sometimes may help a person win large sums of money, but it destroys the habit of hard work and places one's faith in sheer chance. Gambling is also addictive and, as a result, people often lose their wealth and property. When gambling becomes an addiction,

it can cause great strain and tension within a family; and may even destroy it.

*'Al-'Anṣab,* the idolatry is a form of *Shirk* and is a major sin in Islam. The idolatry is the worship of idols, images or other creations of Allah (SWT). Some people worship idols which they make themselves, while others worship such things as rivers, mountains and stars.

Human beings are the best creation of Allah (SWT) and all things have been created for them. Allah (SWT) says He will forgive every sin except the *Shirk*. As Muslims, we must not worship anyone or anything but Allah (SWT).

*'Al-'Azlām* is the divination or the fortune-telling. Fortune-tellers have invented many ways to tell people their future. Some do so by reading palms, studying the stars, or using birth charts. The Arabs used arrows to predict the future.

Allah (SWT) says that only He has full knowledge of the future. The habit of trusting others for the future shakes our faith in Allah (SWT). A Muslim must work hard and leave the future in Allah's Hands.

The four evils, as stated in this verse, are sicknesses that have plagued society for centuries and continue to do so even today. Even many educated and intelligent people indulge in these evils and, as a result, slowly lose control over their lives. A Muslim must lead a healthy life and help others to overcome these works of *Shaiṭān*.

## WE HAVE LEARNED:

* Drinking, gambling, idolatry and fortune-telling are the works of *Shaiṭān*.
* Islam completely forbids these evils.
* A Muslim must lead his life according to Islamic principles and invite others to do the same.

## DO WE KNOW THESE WORDS?

addictive
*'Al-'Anṣab*
*'Al-Khamr*
*'Al-Maisir*
*'Al-'Azlām*
divination
fortune-telling
numb

Lesson 23

# Senseless Actions

بِسْمِ اللهِ الرَّحْمٰنِ الرَّحِيمِ

وَالَّذِينَ لَا يَشْهَدُونَ الزُّورَ

وَإِذَا مَرُّوا بِاللَّغْوِ مَرُّوا كِرَامًا

*Wa-alladhīna lā yashhadūna-(a)z-zūra,*
*wa-'idhā marrū bi-(a)l-laghwi*
*marrū kirāmā*

"And those who will not witness falsehood;
and when they pass by senseless actions,
they pass by with self-respect..."
*('Al-Furqān 25:72)*

EXPLANATION:

In this verse, the term "senseless action" refers to those actions which serve no real purpose, such as backbiting, making fun of others, or showing off. If we find ourselves in such situations, we must leave in a quiet and dignified manner and not in an arrogant, self-righteous way.

If we are laughed at by others, we must not show our anger. We should not return the bad language used against us with equally bad language. If the evil people wish to involve us in a fight, we must leave quietly and not lower ourselves to their standards.

Through senseless actions one wastes his precious time in doing those things that benefit no one. Senseless actions hurt everyone. They lead to mischief and fights.

If we see any of our friends or family members involved with such bad company, we should talk to them and advise them against being friends with such people. We must try to persuade them to act righteously. We should tell them that senseless actions merely serve to hurt others and we are taught never to hurt others intentionally.

As Muslims, we must always be truthful and seek the company of the truthful. We must not be witness to falsehood. Sometimes, people tell lies to get something that they desire. As true Muslims, we neither tell lies nor support the lies of others.

To be a witness to senseless actions is to be part of such actions. Some people may not take part in such actions, but may watch them with interest. In watching there is always danger of involvement.

The evil people may like to get our support for their actions. They may even try to provoke us and pick a fight. If we cannot stop such senseless action, then the best course for us is to leave the scene of such action, we must always avoid the company of such evil people.

## Good and Bad Speech

Rasūlullāh (S) has described for us
the speech of two kinds of people:

A Servant of Allah utters words
which are pleasing to Allah,
and he himself does not give any
importance to that, but Allah honors him
and raises him high because of that.
Another servant of Allah says words
which are dispersing to Allah,
and he himself does not pay any attention
to it, Allah dishonors him and throws
him into the fire because of that.
*('Al-Bukhārī)*

## WE HAVE LEARNED:

* A true Believer does not lie or support falsehood.
* He always avoids senseless actions.
* He always keeps away from bad company.

## DO WE KNOW THESE WORDS?

decent
dignified
falsehood
hostility
senseless action
self-righteous

Lesson 24

# Feeling of Superiority

بِسْمِ اللهِ الرَّحْمٰنِ الرَّحِيْمِ

فَلَا تُزَكُّوٓا۟ أَنفُسَكُمْ هُوَ أَعْلَمُ بِمَنِ ٱتَّقَىٰٓ

*Fa-lā tuzakkū 'anfusa-kum Huwa a'alamu bi-mani-(a)t-taqā*

"Therefore, do not try to prove yourselves pure,
He is best aware of him who guards against evil.
*('An-Najm 53:32)*

When doing a good deed a Believer's intention must always be to please Allah (SWT). A Believer must always seek his reward from Allah (SWT). A Believer must always act right and must keep his intention pure.

There are some people who do good deeds to show off or to gain some kind of material benefits. They are overly proud of their achievements and sometimes even become disdainful of others. They boastfully brag about their achievement. Such people feel that they are superior to others.

As human beings, we are responsible for all our actions. Whatever actions we do are known to Allah (SWT). If we do righteous actions, they are done with Guidance from Allah (SWT). If we do an evil deed, it is done with His Knowledge.

In Islam the intention behind our deeds is always very important. Rasūlullāh (S) taught us:

> "Actions are determined by the intention.
> Everyone gets the reward for what he intends for."
> *('Al-Bukhārī)*

These people think that they may do what they want with their possessions. They use these gifts of Allah (SWT) for their own benefit and glory. They wish to be praised for everything they do. Instead of being thankful to Allah (SWT) for providing His many Blessings, their success and achievements make them proud and arrogant.

The more people achieve success, the more they are likely to believe in their own merit and forget about the Mercy of Allah (SWT). They do not realize that one day, they will die and the only thing that will help them then is their good faith and actions.

Allah (SWT) commands us to be sincere in all our actions and to do things to please Allah (SWT) alone. The Qur'ān warns us against bragging, even about our good deeds. The true knowledge of what is good and what is bad is contained in the Qur'ān and the *Sunnah* of our Prophet (S). Keeping the company of the righteous people and following their good example will guide us on the Right Path.

Allah (SWT) knows both our intentions and actions. We must act righteously with sincere intentions. The Qur'ān advises us:

وَقُلِ ٱعْمَلُوا۟ فَسَيَرَى ٱللَّهُ عَمَلَكُمْ وَرَسُولُهُۥ وَٱلْمُؤْمِنُونَ ۖ
وَسَتُرَدُّونَ إِلَىٰ عَٰلِمِ ٱلْغَيْبِ وَٱلشَّهَٰدَةِ
فَيُنَبِّئُكُم بِمَا كُنتُمْ تَعْمَلُونَ

And say (O Muḥammad to Believers)
" Do your deeds, Allah will look to your actions,
and will His Messenger and the Believers,
and you will be brought back to the Knower
of the invisible and visible, and He will
tell you what you used to do."
*(At-Tawbah 9:105)*

## WE HAVE LEARNED:

* All the actions of the believers must be to please Allah (SWT).
* A Believer must not be proud of his actions and must not feel superior to others.
* We must always seek true knowledge and the company of the righteous people.

## DO WE KNOW THESE WORDS?

bragging
disdainful
intention
righteous
feeling superior

# Lesson 25

# Making Mischief

بِسْمِ اللَّهِ الرَّحْمَٰنِ الرَّحِيمِ

إِنَّ ٱللَّهَ لَا يُحِبُّ ٱلْمُفْسِدِينَ

*'Inn(a)-Allāha lā yuḥibbu-(a)l-mufsidīn*

Indeed, Allah does not love those
who make corruption.
*('Al-Qaṣaṣ 28:77)*

EXPLANATION:

Islam is a religion of peace. The word Islam comes from the same root as *Salām,* which in Arabic means "peace." Islam teaches all human beings not to create mischief and to live peacefully with one another. Peace is only possible when we respect each other.

Most people in society want to live peacefully and work together for common good. However, every society has a few mischief makers who try to corrupt the society with their evil designs. Such people do not respect the rights of others. They create many problems with their evil doing. They fight and argue among themselves and with others. Instead of following the instructions of Allah (SWT) by enjoining good and forbidding evil, they spread corruption and dissention throughout the society.

These evil people oppress the weak and do not help the orphans, the widows or the needy. They do not think twice about harming, or sometimes even killing others to get what they want. They break the Laws of Allah (SWT) and the rules of the society.

Such people steal, cheat, commit crimes and spread violence. Sometimes these evil people organize themselves into powerful groups. They make the lives of innocent people miserable. Sometimes even the police or governments find it hard to break their power. The government and the society have to work together to destroy the power of these evil people. Sometimes even governments come under the control of these evil people.

This power makes them proud and arrogant. They use their power to oppress the weak and to deprive people of their natural rights.

Whether an individual, a group or an entire government, the evil people are always defeated. Allah (SWT) dislikes the evil-doer and mischief maker. Good people must always work together to establish justice and remove corruption from the land. When we fight against evil the help of Allah (SWT) is always with us.

Allah (SWT) will punish these people for their evil deeds. He may allow them the freedom to do as they please in this world for a short while but finally they will be defeated.

## The End of Mischief Maker

Once Rasūlullāh (S) asked his *Ṣaḥābah,* "Who is a poor person?" They replied, "The one who has no money." He then said, "In fact, the real poor person in my *'Ummah* will be one who will come on the Day of Judgment with his *Ṣalāh, Ṣiyām* and *Zakāh.* And in the world he swore at someone, accused someone, usurped someone wealth, killed someone, hurt someone, then all his good actions will be divided among his victims. And if his good deeds are exhausted but the compensation of his victims remain, he will receive the bad deeds of the victim and will be thrown into Hell.

*(Muslim)*

## WE HAVE LEARNED:

* The mischief-makers make trouble for everyone.
* Allah (SWT) does not like those who make mischief.
* Those who spread corruption and evil will be punished in the Hereafter.

## DO WE KNOW THESE WORDS?

corruption
forbidden
generate
mischief
natural rights
oppress

# Lesson 26

# Making Fun of Others

بِسْمِ اللهِ الرَّحْمٰنِ الرَّحِيْمِ

يَٰٓأَيُّهَا ٱلَّذِينَ ءَامَنُوا۟ لَا يَسْخَرْ قَوْمٌ مِّن قَوْمٍ
عَسَىٰٓ أَن يَكُونُوا۟ خَيْرًا مِّنْهُمْ
وَلَا نِسَآءٌ مِّن نِّسَآءٍ
عَسَىٰٓ أَن يَكُنَّ خَيْرًا مِّنْهُنَّ

*Ya 'ayyuha-(a)lladhīna 'āmanū la yaskhar qawmun min*
*qawmin 'asā 'an yakūnū khairan min-hum*
*wa-la nisa' un min nisa' in*
*'asā 'an yakunna khairan min-hunna*

Oh Believers! Let not one community
make fun of another community.
It may be that it (the latter) be better than (the former).
Nor let some women make fun of other women.
It may be that the (latter) be better than the (former).
*('Al-Ḥujurāt 49:11)*

EXPLANATION:

Everyone in human society deserves respect from others. Societies are comprised of people who are different from each other. Often times, the differences in color, race, language, culture, religion and appearance makes us feel mistrustful of one another. This feeling sometimes gives rise to hostility and enemity toward those who do not belong to one's group.

In this verse, Allah (SWT) warns those who discriminate against and make fun of others. Some people think that they are superior to others by birth and use these false beliefs to promote racism and hatred between different communities. History is full of examples of one group of people depriving another of its basic rights. In some extreme cases, one people enslave others because of their religious, cultural or racial differences.

There are some people who are born physically or mentally handicapped. These are very special people. They need our sympathy, help and support. Sometimes, ignorant people make fun of them and by doing so, they hurt their feelings.

They do not know how dear these handicapped people are to Allah (SWT).

The Qur'ān teaches us that no person has a right to make fun of others. No man or woman must think that he or she is better than another person. No nation or race can claim that they are better than others. As human beings we are the same and it is only our faith and actions that make us better or worse before Allah (SWT).

As Muslims, we must have tolerance for all people, regardless of how different they may be from us. We must realize that we are all creatures of Allah (SWT), and therefore, we should never criticize any individual about their physical appearance or position.

We must respect the languages, customs, and beliefs of others, just as we would like them to respect ours. Even our differences in religious beliefs should not lead us to laughing at each other and fighting. We should try to know, understand, and respect one another. The Qur'ān teaches us that we are children of the same parents, 'Ādam (A) and Ḥawwā' (R), and thus, of the same family.

Allah (SWT) has created humankind into many nations, communities, tribes, races, and colors. Though we are created with different appearances, we are all created equal and with equal rights. As human beings we must accept our differences and show respect for each other.

## WE HAVE LEARNED:

* We should not make fun of others if they are different from us.

* No group of people should discriminate against another group because we are all created equal.

* We are all children of the same parents, 'Ādam (A) and Ḥawwā' (R) and deserve the same respect.

## DO WE KNOW THESE WORDS?

discriminate
estranged
race
tribe

# Lesson 27

# Suspicion and Spying

بِسْمِ اللَّهِ الرَّحْمَٰنِ الرَّحِيمِ

يَٰٓأَيُّهَا ٱلَّذِينَ ءَامَنُوا۟ ٱجْتَنِبُوا۟ كَثِيرًا مِّنَ ٱلظَّنِّ
إِنَّ بَعْضَ ٱلظَّنِّ إِثْمٌ ۖ وَلَا تَجَسَّسُوا۟

*Yā 'ayyuha-(a)lladhīna 'āmanū-(i)jtanibū kathīran mina (a)ẓ-ẓanni, 'inna ba'ḍ aẓ-ẓanni 'ithmun, wa-lā-tajassasū....*

Oh Believers! Avoid suspicion as much (as possible), for suspicion in some cases is a sin, and spy not on one another...
*('Al-Ḥujurāt 49:12)*

EXPLANATION:

As Muslims, we must respect other human beings and their intentions. Even if we do not understand other people's beliefs or actions, we have no right to make assumptions about them. Suspicion is assuming negative things about a person, without actually having any proof. Suspicious individuals often mistrust people's motives or actions, especially if they do not know them well.

Suspicion is often caused by our ignorance of other peoples actions and intentions. It very often has no foundation in reality, and it causes unnecessary hatred and enmity between people.

Spying is trying to secretly uncover information about other people that they would like to keep private. Sometimes people spy on others because they are suspicious of other people's intentions or because they want information that they can use against that person. Some people just spy on others as a means of enjoyment.

People spy on others by listening in on conversations, by secretly watching them, or by reading their letters and private papers. Also, these days there are many electronic devices that enable people to monitor others.

We have many private thoughts or personal problems that we would like to keep to ourselves. There are other things that we want to share only with our family and close friends. If anyone else discovers these private matters, we feel uncomfortable. Similarly, others feel bad if we try to discover their secrets. In Islam, it is sinful to spy on others in order to learn their private affairs.

Those who are known to spy are mistrusted and held in suspicion by others. They have no respect among their friends. If we are not suspicious of others and do not have bad ideas about them, we will not gain pleasure from learning their private affairs.

Some time we learn about others private affairs by accident. We must keep all such information to ourselves. Those who respect others earn respect for themselves. Every-one has a right to their privacy and no one should try to intentionally disturb it.

## True Meaning of Islam

Some people in the West are suspicious of Muslims. Islam and Muslims are often portrayed in the media as violent and supportive of terrorism. If they had knowledge of the true teachings of Islam, they would see that their suspicions have no basis. Muslims have a special responsibility to lead their life according to Islamic teachings and be model citizens in every respect. We should teach everyone the true meaning of Islam.

## WE HAVE LEARNED:

* We should respect others and not be suspicious of them.
* We must not spy on others.
* Everyone has a right to privacy.

## DO WE KNOW THESE WORDS?

assumptions
electronically
to monitor
motive
suspicion

Lesson

28

# Defaming

بِسْمِ اللَّهِ الرَّحْمَٰنِ الرَّحِيمِ

وَلَا تَلْمِزُوٓا۟ أَنفُسَكُمْ وَلَا تَنَابَزُوا۟ بِٱلْأَلْقَٰبِ ۖ
بِئْسَ ٱلِٱسْمُ ٱلْفُسُوقُ بَعْدَ ٱلْإِيمَٰنِ ۚ
وَمَن لَّمْ يَتُبْ فَأُو۟لَٰٓئِكَ هُمُ ٱلظَّٰلِمُونَ

*Wa-lā talmizū 'anfusa-kum wa-lā-tanābazū bi-(a)l-'alqāb(i),*
*bi'sa-(a)l-'ismu-(a)l-fusūqu ba'da-(A)l-'īmāni*
*wa-man lam-yatub fa-'ulā'ika humu-(a)ẓ-ẓālimūn*

Do not defame, nor be sarcastic to one another,
ill-seeming is the name connoting wickedness,
(to be used of one) after he has believed:
And those who do not desist are indeed doing wrong.
*('Al-Ḥujurāt 49:11)*

EXPLANATION:

Allah (SWT) has created us all equals. All human beings are of the same family. We are all creations of Allah (SWT) and descendants of 'Ādam (A) and Ḥawwā' (R). Therefore, we are children of the same parents. Many people do not realize this, and, as a result, they make fun of each other and hate each other.

Human beings are created in tribes, nations and have different colors and speak many different languages. Individual human beings are also created different from one another. Each one has his/her own color, taste, feelings and characteristics.

Sometimes when we do not understand each other, we try to find fault in the other person. It is always easy to find fault with others. Sometimes we blame others for our own mistakes. Sometimes we accuse others if something bad happens to us.

When people and communities develop the habit of blaming others for their own faults, they do not improve. When people or communities make mistakes, they must look to their own mistakes and should try to correct them. Once a mistake is recognized and corrected, people progress and do better.

It is also easy to criticize others in everything that they do. If a person does not belong to our group, we criticize him and do not expect any good to come out of him. Even if he does something good, we still find fault with him.

All criticism, however, is not bad. Sometimes, criticism is given to improve our action. Such a criticism is a blessing. The criticism which ridicules people, calls them names and makes fun of them is wrong.

Islam is a religion for everyone. No one person or group is preferred over the other person or group. Even enemies become friends after they accept Islam. Allah (SWT) forgives their former sins.

If someone accepts Islam, he or she must be treated with great respect and love. It is wrong to remind them of their past bad deeds or blame them for what they did in the past.

We should not blame people, ridicule them or call them names. We should respect everyone in spite of our differences with them.

## WE HAVE LEARNED:

* We should not blame or be sarcastic to others or call them by evil names.
* We cannot improve if we blame others for our faults.
* The criticism made to improve a situation must be done in a decent manner.

## DO WE KNOW THESE WORDS?

defame
characteristics
progress
criticize
criticism

Lesson 29

# Backbiting

بِسْمِ اللّٰهِ الرَّحْمٰنِ الرَّحِيْمِ

وَلَا يَغْتَب بَّعْضُكُم بَعْضًا
أَيُحِبُّ أَحَدُكُمْ أَن يَأْكُلَ لَحْمَ أَخِيهِ مَيْتًا
فَكَرِهْتُمُوهُ وَاتَّقُوا اللَّهَ
إِنَّ اللَّهَ تَوَّابٌ رَّحِيمٌ

*Wa-lā tajassasū wa-lā-yaghtab ba'ḍu-kum ba'ḍan,*
*'ayuḥibbu 'aḥadu-kum 'an-ya'kula laḥma 'akhī-hi maitan*
*fa-karihtumū-hu, wa-(a)t-taqū-(A)llāha*
*'inna-(A)llāha Tawwābun Raḥīm(un).*

And neither spy on one another, nor backbite one another.
Would anyone of you like to eat the flesh of his dead brother?
No, you would hate to do it; and fear Allah;
Indeed! Allah is Oft-Returning and Most-Merciful.
*('Al-Ḥujurāt 49: 12)*

EXPLANATION:

The Qur'ān forbids two major evils of human society: spying and backbiting. Spying has been discussed in a previous chapter, therefore here, we will concentrate on backbiting.

Backbiting is to say mean or spiteful things about someone who is absent. This is wrong because that person cannot defend himself against the accusations or false statements made about him. In his absence, an innocent person may be accused of things that he never actually did. Backbiting hurts the good name of a person and makes him look bad before other people.

Most people backbite others for fun. They laugh at the expense of others. It is always easy to laugh at someone who is not present. Sometimes people backbite out of spite. If they do not like a person, they do not want anyone to like that person either.

Backbiting is an act very much disliked by Allah (SWT) and

His Messenger (S). In fact, the Qur'ān compares it to the eating of the flesh of one's dead brother! Brothers have such a deep love for one another that they would hate to see the other hurt even in a minor way. How unthinkable it is to eat the flesh of a brother. Worse still is the idea of eating the flesh of one's dead brother. Thus, this comparison is made to emphasize the seriousness of this evil act.

It is bad enough to criticize people and make fun of them in their presence, but to do so behind their back is a much more despised act.

> Once Rasūlullāh (S) asked his *Ṣaḥābah,* "Do you know what backbiting is?"
>
> They respectfully replied, "Allah and His Messenger know the best."
>
> Rasūlullāh (S) then said, "Backbiting is to talk about your brother in a way that he would not like."
>
> The *Ṣaḥābah* asked, "Even if what I say is found in my brother?"
>
> "Even if that be true," replied Rasūlullāh (S), "that is backbiting; if that is not true that will be a lie."
> *(Mishkāt)*

A false accusation against an innocent person is worse than backbiting.

## WE HAVE LEARNED:

* Spying on others and backbiting are two very bad habits.
* An absent person cannot defend himself against the accusations.
* Backbiting is extremely bad, it is compared to eating the flesh of one's dead brother.

## DO WE KNOW THESE WORDS?

accusation
backbiting
*Kidhb*
privacy
recognize
reputation

# Lesson 30

# Boasting

بِسْمِ اللهِ الرَّحْمٰنِ الرَّحِيْمِ

وَلَا تُصَعِّرْ خَدَّكَ لِلنَّاسِ
وَلَا تَمْشِ فِي ٱلْأَرْضِ مَرَحًا
إِنَّ ٱللَّهَ لَا يُحِبُّ كُلَّ مُخْتَالٍ فَخُورٍ

*Wa-lā tuṣa''ir khadda-ka li-(a)n-nāsi*
*wa-lā tamshi fi-(a)l-'arḍi maraḥa,*
*'inna-(A)llāha lā yuḥibbu kulla mukhtālin fakhūr(in)*

And swell not your cheek toward people,
nor walk with arrogance on Earth;
for Allah does not love any proud boaster.
*(Luqmān 31:18)*

EXPLANATION:

Allah (SWT) loves people who are humble and modest. Allah (SWT) does not like arrogant and boastful people. Arrogant people think that they are superior to others. They think very highly of themselves and have little respect for other people's ideas and feelings.

Boastful people brag about their own achievements while belittling other people. When they talk to others they are arrogant. Their cheeks are puffed with false pride and self-importance. They walk on this Earth as if they will break it with their weight.

Proud people laugh at other people. They often want to pick a fight with others. They provoke other people and create mischief.

The proud people sometimes group themselves into gangs. The gangs fight each other, spilling blood. Sometimes they go out harming and killing innocent people.

When we see such people, it is our duty to inform them decently that they are acting in an unacceptable manner. We must tell them they are hurting those around them with their arrogant ways.

If they still continue to act in the same way, we know that they are trouble makers and we should not get involved with them. When we are around them, we should remain dignified and should refrain from adopting their bad habits.

If Allah (SWT) has blessed us with youth and good health, we must thank Him. We should use our energies in doing good to others. If Allah (SWT) has honored us with wealth, we must spend it in good cause. If Allah (SWT) has honored us with knowledge, we must use it to promote good ideas.

Being proud of Allah's gifts makes us unworthy of those gifts. We must know Allah (SWT) can withdraw his favors from us at any time. Therefore, while we have these gifts, we must use them properly and thank Allah (SWT) for His Kindness.

## Do Not Walk With Pride, Pride Does Not Help

وَلَا تَمْشِ فِي ٱلْأَرْضِ مَرَحًا

إِنَّكَ لَن تَخْرِقَ ٱلْأَرْضَ

وَلَن تَبْلُغَ ٱلْجِبَالَ طُولًا

*And do not walk on Earth with pride; for you can neither break the Earth, nor you can stretch yourself to the height of the mountains.*

*('Al-'Isrā' 17:37)*

## WE HAVE LEARNED:

* Allah (SWT) does not love proud and arrogant people.

* Proud and boastful people think they are superior to others.

* A self-respecting person does not get involved with such arrogant people.

## DO WE KNOW THESE WORDS?

arrogant
belittling
boastful
dignified
proud
provocation
refrain
self-respecting
superior

Lesson 31

# Miserliness

بِسْمِ ٱللَّهِ ٱلرَّحْمَٰنِ ٱلرَّحِيمِ

وَلَا يَحْسَبَنَّ ٱلَّذِينَ يَبْخَلُونَ بِمَآ ءَاتَىٰهُمُ
ٱللَّهُ مِن فَضْلِهِۦ هُوَ خَيْرًا
لَّهُم ۖ بَلْ هُوَ شَرٌّ لَّهُمْ ۖ سَيُطَوَّقُونَ
مَا بَخِلُوا۟ بِهِۦ يَوْمَ ٱلْقِيَٰمَةِ ۗ

*Wa-lā yaḥsabana-(a)lladhīna yabkhalūna bi-mā 'a'ṭa-hum-u-(A)llāhu min faḍli-hi huwa khairal-la-hum bal huwa sharrul la-hum, sa-yuṭawwaqūna mā bakhilū bi-hī yawma-(a)l-qiyāmah(ti),wa-li-(A)llāhi mīrāthu-(a)s-samāwāti wa-(a)l-'arḍi, wa-(A)llāhu bi-ma ta'malūna Khabīr.*

And let not those who show miserliness in spending of the gifts that Allah has blessed them with, think that it is good for them. No, it is worse for them. That which they hoard (out of miserliness) will be made a twisted collar for them on the Day of Judgment.
*('Al 'Imrān 3:180)*

EXPLANATION:

As Muslims we know that everything we possess is a gift from Allah (SWT). Some of these gifts from Him are free. Allah (SWT) has given us brains, hands, feet, eyes and ears to help us in our daily activities. If we were to lose even one of these free gifts, our life would immediately become more difficult. We should show our thanks to Allah (SWT) for His gifts by being generous to others.

However, many of Allah's gifts need to be worked for, such as wealth, knowledge and friends. We must realize that they are a form of Allah's Blessings upon us. We must spend from the gifts that Allah (SWT) has given us on our families and friends, as well as on those who are in need such as orphans, poor and wayfarers. Allah (SWT) has made the *Zakāh* obligatory on us. The *Zakāh* is a percentage of our wealth that we have saved during the year which must be given to the poor and the needy.

Allah (SWT) also wants us to give the *Ṣadaqah*. The *Ṣadaqah* is charity that we must pay in excess of our *Zakāh*. We must also give gifts of love and friendship to our relatives, friends and the needy.

Rasūlullāh (S) said:

> "Give gifts, it increases love between you."
> *(Musnad 'AbīYa'lā)*

Taking care of one's family, parents and relatives is a responsibility which we all must fulfill. We must also donate money to just and charitable causes such as our Islamic Centers, schools, hospitals, and to charities in general.

Time is one of our most valuable possessions. The most valuable donation we can make to any cause or individual is our time.

Some people wrongly think that by giving money away they will become poor. They feel that by hoarding their wealth and saving their money they will have no worries or troubles. All the wealth of the world belongs to Allah (SWT). It is He Who gives us the opportunity to make a living and it is He Who provides for all our needs. By spending in His Way, we increase our earnings instead of decreasing them. Rasūlullāh (S) said,

> "Allah (SWT) promises, you spend money in charity, I will spend on you."
> *('Al-Bukhārī and Muslim)*

On the Day of Judgment, the money hoarded and saved will be made into a twisted collar and will hang on the neck of the miser, choking him. A generous person, on the other hand, will receive Allah's pleasure and rewards of *Jannah* for his good works.

## WE HAVE LEARNED:

* Everything we possess is a gift from Allah (SWT).
* We must donate to the needy and to charities and other good causes.
* The miser will be punished for his miserliness on the Day of Judgment, while the generous person will be rewarded.

## DO WE KNOW THESE WORDS?

collar
hoarding
miserliness

بِسْمِ اللهِ الرَّحْمٰنِ الرَّحِيْمِ

وَيْلٌ لِّكُلِّ أَفَّاكٍ أَثِيمٍ

*Wailul li-kulli 'affākin 'athīm.*

Woe to each sinful liar.
*('Al-Jāthiyah 45:7)*

EXPLANATION:

Lying is a sin and Allah (SWT) has cursed those who lie. Sinful people use lies to cover up their evil habits. They start by telling small lies but soon develop the habit of lying all the time.

The liars lose the trust of others. When they say something, nobody believes them. Even when they speak the truth, nobody believes them. The liars do not have any real friends.

Everybody trusts truthful people. Rasūlullāh (S) was known as Aṣ-Ṣādiq (the Truthful) by the people of Makkah. They all trusted Rasūlullāh (S) and knew him to be a truthful person. As Muslims, we should follow the *Sunnah* of Rasūlullāh (S) and try to be always truthful.

We must always avoid lies. Some people tell lies to gain some benefit. Some tell lies to harm and hurt others. Some tell lies for the fun of it. We must avoid all kinds of lies. The Qur'ān advises us:

وَٱجْتَنِبُوا۟ قَوْلَ ٱلزُّورِ

And shun the word that is a lie.
*('Al-Ḥajj 22:30)*

People know that a sinful liar does not distinguish between right and wrong . He is willing to do anything that will benefit him. He does not even mind harming his friends or family for the smallest personal gain.

A sinful liar is cursed by Allah (SWT). A person who has been cursed by Allah (SWT) cannot be blessed by anyone. He must either ask for Allah's forgiveness or await His punishment.

## The Signs of a Hypocrite

Rasūlullāh (S) said,
"Whoever has these four habits –
he is a sure hypocrite *(Munāfiq)*. And
whoever has anyone of these habits –
he has one of the characteristics of
hypocrisy. He is advised to give it up.

The four characteristics of a hypocrite are:
– when he is entrusted with a trust,
he embezzles it.
– when he speaks, he tells a lie.
– when he promises, he does not keep it.
– when he has a dispute with someone,
he uses foul language."

*('Al-Bukhārī and Muslim)*

## WE HAVE LEARNED:

* To lie is a sin and Allah (SWT) curses the liars.

* A Muslim must never tell a lie.

* No one trusts a sinful liar.

## DO WE KNOW THESE WORDS?

curse
distinguish
hypocrite
hypocrisy
sinful liar

Lesson 33

# Jealousy

بِسْمِ اللّٰهِ الرَّحْمٰنِ الرَّحِيْمِ

أَمْ يَحْسُدُونَ ٱلنَّاسَ
عَلَىٰ مَآ ءَاتَىٰهُمُ ٱللَّهُ مِن فَضْلِهِۦ

*'Am yaḥsudūna-an-nāsa*
*'ala mā 'ātā-humu-(A)llāhu min faḍli-hī*

Do they feel jealousy toward human beings
for what Allah has given them of His blessings?
*('An- Nisā' 4:54)*

EXPLANATION:

Jealousy is one of the sicknesses of the heart. A jealous person envies others for the things that they have. He does not count the many favors that Allah (SWT) has bestowed upon him. He does not thank Allah (SWT) for His many Blessings that he shares with others. When he receives the Bounties of Allah (SWT), he feels that he deserves them. He credits Allah's Blessings with his own efforts and feels proud of his success.

If someone else achieves success, he is unhappy. Sometimes, he goes further and tries to destroy that person's happiness.

In *Sūrah 'Al-Falaq,* Allah (SWT) teaches us to seek His refuge,

وَمِن شَرِّ حَاسِدٍ إِذَا حَسَدَ

. . .from the jealousy of the jealous person
as he practices jealousy.
*('Al- Falaq 113:5)*

A Believer is always thankful to Allah (SWT) for what he possesses. He feels happy when he sees someone else being favored by Allah (SWT). He looks to the people who are not as blessed as he is, rather than being envious of those who have been blessed with more than himself. When he looks at the people who have more of the favors of Allah (SWT) he feels no ill will or jealousy.

Rasūlullāh (S) has advised us:

"Look to those who are in a less favored
situation and not to those who are in
a more favored condition."
*('Aḥmad 'Ibn Hanbal, Muslim and At-Tirmidhī)*

We must work hard to achieve what we want in life. We cannot achieve success without making a serious effort. We must pray to Allah (SWT) for our success and if we achieve what we want, we must thank Him.

We do this by making a special *Du'ā'* of thanks or by offering special *nawāfil* (optional prayers). However, sharing Allah's Blessings with others is the best form of thanks to Allah (SWT) that we can give.

Allah (SWT) promises:

وَإِذْ تَأَذَّنَ رَبُّكُمْ لَئِن شَكَرْتُمْ لَأَزِيدَنَّكُمْ
وَلَئِن كَفَرْتُمْ إِنَّ عَذَابِي لَشَدِيدٌ

And (remember) when you Lord
proclaimed, "If you are thankful
We shall increase Our Blessings,
and if you are thankless: Indeed!
My punishment is great."
*('Ibrāhīm 14:7)*

## The Fire of Jealousy

Rasūlullāh (S) advises us:
"Save yourself from the jealousy. Indeed!
the jealousy consumes good deeds as the
fire consumes the dry wood."
*('Abū Dāwūd)*

## WE HAVE LEARNED:

* Allah (SWT) does not want us to feel jealous towards others.

* We must be thankful for the favors of Allah (SWT).

* We must look to those people who have been less favored than us.

## DO WE KNOW THESE WORDS?

conscience
deserving
*nawāfil*
thankfulness
achieve

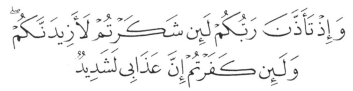

# Lesson 4

| | | | |
|---|---|---|---|
| وَلَا تَقْفُ | And follow not | | |
| مَا لَيْسَ لَكَ بِهِ عِلْمٌ | that of which you have no knowledge | | |
| إِنَّ ٱلسَّمْعَ | for surely, the hearing | وَٱلْبَصَرَ | and the seeing |
| وَٱلْفُؤَادَ | and the heart | كُلُّ أُولَٰٓئِكَ | all these |
| كَانَ عَنْهُ مَسْئُولاً | will be questioned of | | |

# Lesson 5

| | | | |
|---|---|---|---|
| يَٰٓأَيُّهَا ٱلَّذِينَ ءَامَنُوا | O you who believe | قُوٓا أَنْفُسَكُمْ | save yourself |
| وَأَهْلِيكُمْ | and your families | نَارًا | from the fire |
| وَقُودُهَا | whose fuel is | ٱلنَّاسُ | men, people |
| وَٱلْحِجَارَةُ | and stones | | |

# Lesson 6

| | | | |
|---|---|---|---|
| وَءَاتِ | And give | ذَا ٱلْقُرْبَىٰ | the relatives |
| حَقَّهُ | Their due rights | وَٱلْمِسْكِينَ | as to the needy |
| وَٱبْنَ ٱلسَّبِيلِ | and to the traveller | وَلَا تُبَذِّرْ | and waste not your wealth |
| تَبْذِيرًا | in wasteful manner | | |

# Lesson 7

| | | | |
|---|---|---|---|
| وَقَضَىٰ رَبُّكَ | And your Lord commands you | | |
| أَلَّا تَعْبُدُوٓا | to worship none | إِلَّآ إِيَّاهُ | other except Him |
| وَبِٱلْوَٰلِدَيْنِ | to parents | إِحْسَٰنًا | and that you be kind |
| إِمَّا يَبْلُغَنَّ عِندَكَ | reach in your life | ٱلْكِبَرَ | old age |
| أَحَدُهُمَآ | if any one of them | أَوْ كِلَاهُمَا | or both of them |
| فَلَا تَقُل لَّهُمَآ | say not to them | أُفٍّ | a word of contempt |
| وَلَا تَنْهَرْهُمَا | nor rebuke them | وَقُل لَّهُمَا | but speak to them |
| قَوْلًا كَرِيمًا | gracious word | | |

# Lesson 8

| | | | |
|---|---|---|---|
| وَٱلْعَصْرِ | By the Time | إِنَّ ٱلْإِنسَٰنَ | Indeed! man surely |
| لَفِى خُسْرٍ | is in a loss | إِلَّا ٱلَّذِينَ ءَامَنُوا | Except thosse who believe |
| وَعَمِلُوا۟ ٱلصَّٰلِحَٰتِ | and do good works | وَتَوَاصَوْا۟ | and mutually enjoin |
| بِٱلْحَقِّ | (to) truth | بِٱلصَّبْرِ | (to) patience |

# Lesson 9

| | | | |
|---|---|---|---|
| لَا شَرِيكَ لَهُۥ | No partners has He | وَبِذَٰلِكَ | and to this |
| أُمِرْتُ | I was commanded | وَأَنَا۠ | and I am |
| أَوَّلُ ٱلْمُسْلِمِينَ | the first of the Muslims | | |

# Lesson 10

| | | | |
|---|---|---|---|
| وَإِذَا | And when | جَآءَكَ | come to you |
| ٱلَّذِينَ يُؤْمِنُونَ | those who believe | بِـَٔايَٰتِنَا | in Our Signs |
| فَقُلْ | then say | سَلَٰمٌ عَلَيْكُمْ | Peace be upon you |

# Lesson 11

| | | | |
|---|---|---|---|
| وَأَحْسِن | Be kind | كَمَا | as |
| أَحْسَنَ ٱللَّهُ | Allah has been kind | إِلَيْكَ | to you |

# Lesson 12

| | | | |
|---|---|---|---|
| ٱلَّذِينَ يُنفِقُونَ | Those who spend | فِى ٱلسَّرَّآءِ | in time of ease |
| وَٱلضَّرَّآءِ | and in time of difficulty | وَٱلْكَـٰظِمِينَ | and those who control |
| ٱلْغَيْظَ | the anger | وَٱلْعَافِينَ | and are forgiving |
| عَنِ ٱلنَّاسِ | toward people | وَٱللَّهُ | and, Allah |
| يُحِبُّ | loves | ٱلْمُحْسِنِينَ | those who do good |

# Lesson 13

| | | | |
|---|---|---|---|
| يَـٰٓأَيُّهَا ٱلَّذِينَ ءَامَنُوا | O you who believe | ٱصْبِرُوا | show patience |
| وَصَابِرُوا | and be constant | وَرَابِطُوا | and support each other |

# Lesson 14

| | | | |
|---|---|---|---|
| يَـٰٓأَيُّهَا ٱلَّذِينَ ءَامَنُوا | Oh you who believe | كُونُوا قَوَّامِينَ لِلَّهِ | stand out firmly as witnesses to Allah |
| بِٱلْقِسْطِ | in fair dealing | وَلَا يَجْرِمَنَّكُمْ | and let not make you |
| شَنَـَٔانُ قَوْمٍ | the hatred for some people | عَلَىٰٓ أَلَّا تَعْدِلُوا | swerve from justice |
| ٱعْدِلُوا | be just | هُوَ أَقْرَبُ لِلتَّقْوَىٰ | that is next to piety |
| وَٱتَّقُوا ٱللَّهَ | and fear Allah | إِنَّ ٱللَّهَ خَبِيرٌ | Allah is Well-Informed |
| بِمَا تَعْمَلُونَ | of what you do | | |

# *Lesson 15*

يَـٰٓأَيُّهَا ٱلَّذِينَ ءَامَنُوٓا O Believers

| | | | |
|---|---|---|---|
| أَوْفُوا | fulfill | بِٱلْعُقُودِ | the promises |

# *Lesson 16*

| | | | |
|---|---|---|---|
| أَوْفُوا ٱلْكَيْلَ | give just measure | وَلَا تَكُونُوا | and cause no |
| مِنَ ٱلْمُخْسِرِينَ | loss (to others by cheating) | وَزِنُوا | weigh |
| بِٱلْقِسْطَاسِ | with scales | ٱلْمُسْتَقِيمِ | true and upright |
| وَلَا تَبْخَسُوا | and withhold not | ٱلنَّاسَ أَشْيَآءَهُمْ | things due to people |
| وَلَا تَعْثَوْا | and do not spread | فِي ٱلْأَرْضِ مُفْسِدِينَ | mischief in the land |

# *Lesson 17*

| | | | |
|---|---|---|---|
| إِنَّ ٱللَّهَ | Indeed! Allah | يَأْمُرُكُمْ | commands you |
| أَن تُؤَدُّوا | to give back | ٱلْأَمَـٰنَـٰتِ | deposits, trusts |
| إِلَىٰٓ أَهْلِهَا | to their owners | وَإِذَا | and when |
| حَكَمْتُم | you judge | بَيْنَ ٱلنَّاسِ | among people |
| أَن تَحْكُمُوا | to judge | بِٱلْعَدْلِ | with justice |
| إِنَّ ٱللَّهَ | Verily Allah | نِعِمَّا | how excellent |
| يَعِظُكُم | is the teaching He gives you | إِنَّ ٱللَّهَ | Allah is indeed |
| كَانَ سَمِيعًا | Was (and is) Who hears | بَصِيرًا | (and)Who sees everything |

## Lesson 18

| | | | |
|---|---|---|---|
| وَلاَ تَجْعَلْ | And make not | يَدَكَ | your hand |
| مَغْلُولَةً | tied | إِلَىٰ عُنُقِكَ | to your neck |
| وَلاَ تَبْسُطْهَا | nor open it | كُلَّ ٱلبَسْطِ | with a complete opening |
| فَتَقْعُدَ مَلُومًا | so that you are blamed | مَّحْسُورًا | and become regretful |

## Lesson 19

| | | | |
|---|---|---|---|
| مَّثَلُ ٱلَّذِينَ | The example of those | يُنفِقُونَ | who spend |
| أَمْوَالَهُمْ | their wealth | فِى سَبِيلِ ٱللَّهِ | in the way of Allah |
| كَمَثَلِ حَبَّةٍ | is like that of a corn | أَنبَتَتْ | it grew |
| سَبْعَ سَنَابِلَ | seven ears | فِى كُلِّ سُنبُلَةٍ | and in each ear (there is) |
| مِّاْئَةُ حَبَّةٍ | a hundred grains | وَٱللَّهُ | and Allah |

يُضَٰعِفُ لِمَن يَشَاءُ multiply for whom He wishes

وَٱللَّهُ وَاسِعٌ عَلِيمٌ and Allah is Magnanimous and Knowledgable

## Lesson 20

| | | | |
|---|---|---|---|
| وَٱقْصِدْ | and be moderate | فِى مَشْيِكَ | in your walk |
| وَٱغْضُضْ | and lower | مِن صَوْتِكَ | your voice |
| إِنَّ | Indeed | أَنكَرَ ٱلأَصْوَاتِ | the most revolting of all voices |

لَصَوْتُ ٱلحَمِيرِ is the voice (braying) of asses

# Lesson 21

| | | | |
|---|---|---|---|
| وَيُؤثِرُونَ | And they prefer them | عَلَىٰٓ أنفُسِهِمْ | over their own selves |
| وَلَو كَانَ بِهِم | though their lot was | خَصَاصَةٌ | poverty |
| وَمَن يُوقَ | and whoever is saved | شُحَّ | from the greed of |
| نَفْسِهِ | ones own soul | فَأُولَـٰٓئِكَ | then those are the ones |
| هُمُ ٱلْمُفْلِحُونَ | who are successful | | |

# Lesson 22

| | | | |
|---|---|---|---|
| يَـٰٓأَيُّهَا ٱلَّذِينَ ءَامَنُوا | Oh you who believe | إِنَّمَا ٱلْخَمْرُ | Indeed, the intoxicants |
| وَٱلْمَيْسِرُ | the gambling | وَٱلأَنصَابُ | the idols |
| وَٱلأَزْلَـٰمُ | and divining with arrows | رِجْسٌ | are abomination |
| مِّنْ عَمَلِ ٱلشَّيْطَـٰنِ | of Shaitan's work | فَٱجْتَنِبُوهُ | leave it aside |
| لَعَلَّكُمْ تُفْلِحُونَ | that you may succeed | | |

# Lesson 23

| | | | |
|---|---|---|---|
| وَٱلَّذِينَ | And those | لَا يَشْهَدُونَ | who will not witness |
| ٱلزُّورَ | falsehood | وَإِذَا مَرُّوا۟ | and when they pass |
| بِٱللَّغْوِ | by senseless action | مَرُّوا۟ | they pass by |
| كِرَامًا | with self-respect | | |

# Lesson 24

| | | | |
|---|---|---|---|
| فَلَا تُزَكُّوٓا | therefore do not try to commed (praise) | | |
| أَنفُسَكُمْ | yourselves | هُوَ أَعْلَمُ | He is Best Aware |
| بِمَنِ ٱتَّقَىٰٓ | of him who guards against evil | | |

## Lesson 25

| | | | |
|---|---|---|---|
| إِنَّ ٱللَّهَ | Indeed, Allah | لَا يُحِبُّ | does not love those |
| الْمُفْسِدِينَ | who make corruption | | |

## Lesson 26

| | | | |
|---|---|---|---|
| يَٰأَيُّهَا ٱلَّذِينَ ءَامَنُوا | O Believers | لَا يَسْخَرْ | let not make fun of (ridicule, deride) |
| قَوْمٌ | one community | مِّن قَوْمٍ | other community |
| عَسَىٰ | it may be | أَن يَكُونُواْ | that it (latter) be |
| خَيْراً مِّنْهُمْ | better than (former) | وَلَا نِسَآءٌ | Nor let some women |
| مِّن نِّسَآءٍ | of other women | عَسَىٰ | it may be |
| أَن يَكُنَّ | the latter be | خَيْراً | better |
| مِّنْهُنَّ | than the former | | |

## Lesson 27

| | | | |
|---|---|---|---|
| يَٰأَيُّهَا ٱلَّذِينَ ءَامَنُواْ | O Believers | اجْتَنِبُواْ | Avoid |
| كَثِيراً مِّنَ ٱلظَّنِّ | as much as possible of suspicion | إِنَّ بَعْضَ ٱلظَّنِّ | for suspicion in some cases |
| إِثْمٌ | is a sin | وَلَا تَجَسَّسُواْ | and spy not on each other |

## Lesson 28

| | | | |
|---|---|---|---|
| وَلَا تَلْمِزُوٓاْ | Do not defame | أَنفُسَكُمْ | one another |
| وَلَا تَنَابَزُواْ | or be sarcastic | بِٱلْأَلْقَٰبِ | negative neck-naming |
| بِئْسَ | ill seeming (is) | ٱلِاسْمُ | the name |
| الفُسُوقُ | iniquity | بَعْدَ ٱلْإِيمَٰنِ | after having believed |
| وَمَن لَّمْ يَتُبْ | And those who do not desist | فَأُوْلَٰٓئِكَ هُمُ | those are indeed |
| ٱلظَّٰلِمُونَ | doing wrong | | |

# *Lesson 29*

| | | | |
|---|---|---|---|
| وَلَا تَجَسَّسُواْ | And neither spy on each other | وَلَا يَغْتَب | nor backbite |
| بَّعْضُكُم | some of you | بَعْضًا | others |
| أَيُحِبُّ أَحَدُكُمْ | would anyone of you like | أَن يَأْكُلَ | to eat |
| لَحْمَ أَخِيهِ مَيْتًا | the flesh of his dead brother | فَكَرِهْتُمُوهُ | No, you would hate to do it |
| وَٱتَّقُواْ ٱللَّهَ | and fear Allah | إِنَّ ٱللَّهَ | indeed! Allah is |
| تَوَّابٌ رَّحِيمٌ | oft-Returning and Most-Merciful | | |

# *Lesson 30*

| | | | |
|---|---|---|---|
| وَلَاتُصَعِّرْ | And swell not | خَدَّكَ | your cheek (for pride) |
| لِلنَّاسِ | toward people | وَلَا تَمْشِ | nor walk |
| فِى ٱلْأَرْضِ | on earth | مَرَحًا | with arrogance |
| إِنَّ ٱللَّهَ | for Allah | لَا يُحِبُّ | does not love |
| كُلَّ مُخْتَالٍ | any boaster | فَخُورٍ | proud |

# *Lesson 31*

| | | | |
|---|---|---|---|
| وَلَا يَحْسَبَنَّ | and let not those | ٱلَّذِينَ | those who (are) |
| يَبْخَلُونَ | are stingy in spending | بِمَآ ءَاتَـٰهُمُ | of the (gifts) |
| ٱللَّهُ مِن فَضْلِهِ | Allah has blessed them with | هُوَ خَيْرًا لَّهُم | thinking that it is good for them |
| بَلْ هُوَ شَرٌّ لَّهُمْ | rather, it is worse for them | سَيُطَوَّقُونَ | they will be enwraped (as a twisted collar) |
| مَا بَخِلُواْ بِهِ | that which they hoard | يَوْمَ ٱلْقِيَـٰمَةِ | on the Day of Judgment |
| وَلِلَّهِ مِيرَاثُ | to Allah belongs the heritage | ٱلسَّمَـٰوَاتِ وَٱلْأَرْضِ | of heavens and earth |
| وَٱللَّهُ بِمَا تَعْمَلُونَ خَبِيرٌ | and Allah is informed of what you do | | |

# Lesson 32

| | | | |
|---|---|---|---|
| وَيْلٌ | Woe | لِّكُلِّ | to each |
| أَفَّاكٍ | liar | أَثِيمٍ | sinful |

# Lesson 33

| | | | |
|---|---|---|---|
| أَمْ يَحْسُدُونَ | Do they, feel jealousy | ٱلنَّاسَ عَلَىٰ مَآ | toward human beings for what |
| ءَاتَـٰهُمُ ٱللَّهُ | Allah has given them | مِن فَضْلِهِ | of His blessings |

## A

**Abandon:** (n.) to give up, surrender.
**Accusation:** (n.) a charge of offense.
**Achieve:** (v.) to gain by work, to finish.
***'Adab:*** (n.) good manners, decorum, decency.
***'Adl*:** (n.) justice.
**Addictive:** (adj.) to become dependent upon something.
**Agreement:** (n.) understanding; a document containing an understanding.
**'*Akhlaq:*** (n.) morals, morality, nobility of character.
***'Al-Ansab*:** (n.) idols, images, stones placed around the Ka'bah over which the pre-Islamic Arabs used to sacrifice.
**'*Al-'Asr*:** (n.) the Time.
***'Al-'Azlam:*** (n.) arrows without heads and feathers, used in divination, fortune telling.
***Al-Barakah:*** (n.) the Blessing.
***Al-Khamr*:** (n.) wine, alcoholic beverages, liquor.
***Al-Maisir:*** (n.) an ancient Arabian game of chance, played with arrows without heads and feathering, for stakes of slaughtered and quartered animals, game of chance.
**(The) '*Amanah*:** (n.) the Trust.
**'*Anbiya:*** (n.) prophets, plural of Nabi.
**'*Ansar:*** (n.) supporters.
**Appreciate:** (v.) to be grateful for.
**Argument:** (n.) controversy.
**Arrogance:** (n.) being proud.
**Arrogant:** (adj.) greatening one's own importance.
***Ar-Risalah:*** (n.) the Message brought by a messenger, the mission of a prophet.
***'As-Salamu 'Alaikum:*** (n.) Islamic greetings, in Arabic it means "Peace be upon you."
**Aspect:** (n.) appearance, look.
**Assumptions:** (n) anything taken for granted.

## B

**Backbiting:** (v.) to say mean things about someone who is absent.
**Balanced:** (v.) to arrange so that one set of elements equals another.

**Barakah:** (n.) blessing.
**Blessing:** (n.) favor, reward, barakah.
**Boastful:** (adj.) given to praising oneself in order to show off, having arrogance.
**Bragging:** (v.) to show off, to talk big about oneself.

## C

**Characteristic:** (n.) the basic quality or trait of anything.
**Charity:** (n.) doing good to others, donating money, food or clothes to both poor or to a good cause.
**Citadel:** (n.) a fortress protecting a city.
**Civilized:** (adj.) refined, orderly.
**Collar:** (n) a band worn around the neck or the neckline of a garment.
**Commitment:** (n.) to pledge,to put into charge.
**(In) Confidence:** (n.) trust in secrecy.
**Consume:** (v.) to use; to spend wastefully.
**Contempt:** (n.) the act of showing hatred.
**Contribution:** (n.) an offer to help, to assist.
**Convenient:** (adj.) personal comfort, easy.
**Conversation:** (n.) talking with others on some topics.
**Corruption:** (n.) to make evil, cheating.
**Courtesy:** (n.) polite behavior.
**Covenant:** (n.) agreement, legal contract.
**Criticism:** (n.) the act of finding fault, showing disapproval.
**Criticize:** (v.) to blame someone, to point out the faults in something.
**Curse:** (n.) a prayer for harm to come upon someone.

## D

**Dealing:** (n.) a way of doing business.
**Deceive:** (v.) to deal with dishonesty.
**Decent:** (adj.) good taste.
**Defame:** (v.) to destroy someone's reputation by slander.
**Descent:** (n.) decline.
**Deserving:** (adj.) to be worthy of.
**Different:** (adj.) not the same.
**Differentiate:** (v.) state the difference, to show that something is not similar, to distinguish.
**Dignified:** (adj.) showing honor to someone.

**Discriminate:** (v.) to note differences among two groups, to prefer one over the other.
**Disdainful:** (adj.) to be full of hate
**Distinguish:** (v.) to recognize by some marks or characteristics.
**Divining:** (v.) prophecizing, to infer spiritually.
***Dua'*:** (v,) supplication, calling upon God.

## E

**Electronically:** (adv.) anything that relates to electronics such as radio, T. V. etc.
**Equality:** (n.) same, identical.
**Estranged:** (v.) to lose the affective or confidence of someone.
**Evolve:** (v.) to develop gradually.
**Exclusive:** (adj.) reserved for particular persons.

## F

**Facilitate:** (v.) to make easier.
**Faculties:** (n.) a physical function; ie, the five main senses.
**Falsehood:** (n.) the practice of lying.
**Forbidden:** (adj.) commanded against doing something.
**Fortunate:** (adj.) lucky.
**Fortune-telling:** (v,) telling the future.

## G

**Generate:** (v.) to produce.
**Generous:** (adj.) giving.
**Gratitude:** (n.) thankfulness.
**Greetings:** (n.) best wishes, regards.
**Guidance:** (n.) advice, direction.

## H

***Halal*:** (v.) permitted by religious law.
***Haram*:** (v.) prohibited by religious law.
**Hardship:** (n.) suffering.
***Hawwa*:** (pro.n.) Eve.
**Hoard:** (n.) hidden accumulation of wealth.
**Hoarding:** (v.) to hold something from the market to sell it at a higher price later.

**Hostility:** (n.) unfriendly conduct.
**Humble:** (adj.) not proud, modest.
**Humility:** (n.) the act of being humble.

## I

**Imposed:** (v.) to establish anything by authority.
**Injustice:** (n.) an unfair act or deed.
**Intention:** (n.) thought of doing something.
**Interaction:** (n.) action involving more than one person.
**Investment:** (n.) money put away for income or profit.

## J

**Justice:** (n.) the administration of what is fair, *'Adl.*

## K

***Khalifah*:** (n.) vicegerent, successor.
**(The) *Khiyanah*:** (n.) treachery, treason, deception, embezzlement.

## M

**Manners:** (n.) social conduct, behavior.
**Merit:** (n.) a praiseworthy quality.
**Mischief:** (n.) action that annoys.
**Miser:** (n.) a person who does not spend his money.
**Miserliness:** (n.) the act of being a miser.
**Moderation:** (n.) the act of avoiding extremes, balancing.
**(To) Monitor:** (v.) to watch or observe.
**Moral:** (n.) rules, regulations and teachings about how to be a good person.
**Motive:** (n.) moving to action, purpose.
***Muhajirin*:** (n.) emigrants, the *Sahabah* who migrated from Makkah to Madinah.

## N

***Nawafil:*** ( *Nafl* sing.) special optional prayers, not *fard.*
**Numb:** (adj.) lacking sensation or emotion.

## O

**Obligation:** (n.) duty to do an act.
**Oppress:** (v.) to crush by abuse or power.
**Oppression:** (n.) unjust or cruel exercise of power.

## P

**Patience:** (n.) to endure without complaining.
**Prescribed:** (v.) to lay down as a guide or rule of action.
**Pride:** (n.) to have a high opinion of oneself.
**Privacy:** (n.) secrecy.
**Private:** (adj.) personal.
**Progress:** (v.) improve, advance.
**Proud:** (adj.) showing excessive self-esteem, highly pleased.
**Provocation:** (n.) something that arouses anger.
**Purpose:** (n.) intention, resolution.

## Q

***Qist:*** (n.) justice, fairness, equity.

## R

**Race:** (n.) a group of people united on the basis of common history, color, nationality, or geographic distribution.
***Rahmatun li (a) l-'Alamin:*** (adj.) Mercy to Mankind, title of *Rasulallah* in the Qur'an.
**Recognize:** (v.) identify.
**Reputation:** (n.) status, honor, dignity, prestige.
**Righteous:** (adj.) one who tries to do things religiously, morally and correctly.
**Righteousness:** (n.) the quality of being morally right, always doing right acts.
**Rebuke:** (v.) to criticize sharply.
**Recommend:** (v.) to speak well of, to support someone for a position.
**Respect:** (n.) a feeling of honor for someone, approval, and liking.
**Respond:** (v.) answer, reply.
**Responsibility:** (n.) charge, duty, obligation, commitment
**Retaliate:** (v.) to return like for like, especially to return an unfriendly or hostile action with a similar one.
***Rasul:*** (n.) Messenger.

## S

**Sacrifice:** (v.) to offer something to Allah (SWT); to give something away dear to you for some person or cause.

***Sadaqah*:** (n.) an act of charity, anything we give beyond *Zakah*.

***Sadaqah Jariah*:** (n.) a continuing (recurring, perpetual) charity.

***Sahabah:*** (n.) the companions of the Prophet (S), plural of *Sahabi*.

**Secret:** (n.) something kept hidden from others or known only to oneself or to a few; a mystery.

**Self-respecting:** (adj.) properly valuing oneself, having respect for oneself.

**Self-righteous:** (adj.) to think of oneself as right, moralistic.

**Self-sacrifice:** (n.) sacrifice of one's personal interests or well-being for the sake of others or for a cause.

**Senseless action:** (n.) meaningless act or deed, a work that does not make sense.

**Society:** (n.) a group of people united in a relationship and having some interest, activity, or purpose in common

**Spy:** (v.) to observe or listen in secret to obtain information.

**Submission:** (n.) the act of submitting or surrendering to the power of another.

**Superior:** (adj.) located higher than another; upper.

**Suspicion:** (n.) the act of suspecting something.

**Sympathetic:** (adj.) understanding the needs, feelings, problems, and views of others.

## T

***Tawhid:*** (n.) The Oneness of Allah (SWT).

***Tayyib:*** (adj.) good, pure.

**Thankfulness:** (n.) appreciation, gratitude, gratefulness.

**Tribe:** (n.) a group of people sharing common ancestry.

## U

**Upright:** (adj.) adhering strictly to moral principles; righteous.

## V

**Vicegerent:** (n.) person exercising delegated power.

**Virtue:** (n.) goodness, moral excellence and righteousness.

**Virtuous:** (adj.) quality of excellence.

# W

***Wa-'Alai-kum As-Salam*:** In Arabic it means "And upon you be Peace." When somebody greets us in return we say *"Wa-'Alai-kum As-Salam."*

***Wa-Barakatu-hu:*** "And His (Allah's) Blessings."

***Wa Rahmat Allah:*** "And the Mercy of God."

**Witness:** (n.) someone who sees something occur.

**Worldly:** (adj.) knowledgeable in the ways of the world; sophisticated.

**Wronged:** (v.) treated unjustly.

## INTRODUCING THE AUTHORS

Dr. Abidullah Ghazi, Executive Director of IQRA' International, and his wife, Dr. Tasneema Ghazi, Director of Curriculum, are co–founders of IQRA' International Educational Foundation (a non–profit Islamic educational trust established in 1983) and Chief Editors of its educational program. They have combined their talents and expertise and, for the last two decades, dedicated their lives to produce a Comprehensive Program of Islamic Studies for our children and youth and to develop IQRA' into a major center of research and development for Islamic Studies, specializing in Islamic education.

**Abidullah Ghazi,** M. A. (Alig), M. Sc. Econ. (LSE London), Ph. D. (Harvard)

Dr. Abidullah Ghazi, a specialist in Islamic Studies and Comparative Religion, belongs to a prominent family of the Ulama' of India. His family has been active in the field of Islamic education, *dawah*, and struggle for freedom. Dr. Ghazi's early education was carried in traditional *Madāris*. He has studied at Muslim University, Aligarh, The London School of Economics, and Harvard University. He has taught at the Universities of Jamia Millia Islamia, Delhi, London, Harvard, San Diego, Minnesota, Northwestern, Governors State and King Abdul Aziz (Jeddah). He is a consultant for the development of the program of Islamic Studies in various schools and universities. He is a well–known community worker, speaker, writer and poet.

**Tasneema K. Ghazi,** M. A. (Alig), M. Ed. (Allahabad), Acd. Dip. (London), CAGS (Harvard), Ph. D. (Minnesota)

Dr. Tasneema Ghazi is a specialist in Child Development and Reading (Curriculum and Instruction). She has studied at the Universities of Aligarh, Allahabad, London, Harvard, San Diego, and Minnesota. She has taught in India, England, Saudi Arabia, and the United States at various levels: kindergarten, elementary, junior, senior and university. Since her arrival in the USA in 1968, she has been involved with the schools of Islamic Studies providing them valuable advice and guidance. Working with children is her main interest.

Dr. and Mrs. Ghazi have a life–long commitment to write, develop and produce Islamic educational material and quality textbooks at various levels. Dr. Tasneema Ghazi has completed Pre–school and Kindergarten Curricula and plans to produce an integrated curriculum from pre–school to high school by 1998, *Insha Allah*.

Their textbooks on the *Sīrah* and other Islamic subjects have become standard textbooks in Islamic schools in USA and all across the world, and are being published in several parts of the world and translated in major languages of the world.

They have five children, Bushra, Rashid, Saba' and twins, Suhaib and Usama. Their children provided them with their first experimental lab. They are also their co–workers.